MURDER
IN EDINBURGH

KEiTH WiNToN

Edinburgh
Impressions

Printed in Great Britain by
Thomson Litho Ltd, East Kilbride, Scotland

First published in Great Britain in 1985 by
Edinburgh Impressions
6c Dryden Street
Edinburgh EH7 4QB   ISBN   0 951 0099 2 3

FOREWORD

Edinburgh is justly proud of its long history which has been recounted by many authors. Most of them have outlined the parts played by the city's famous and illustrious sons and daughters. However, like all centres of human activity and endeavour, Edinburgh has had its darker aspects which have received less attention, unless they have become famous because of the degree of outrage caused by the infamy concerned. Such characters as Deacon Brodie and Burke and Hare most obviously spring to mind. And yet, an odd facet of the human make-up is to harbour a prurient fascination, on occasions bordering on admiration, for the seamier side of human behaviour. So, why the wish to keep such tales hidden away from view?

In the first of a series of recollections of the more criminal events in Edinburgh's history, we have concentrated on the crime of murder. It is a crime which appears to attract morbid curiosity. Part of its attraction is perhaps its classless aspect, affecting the highest in the land to the most lowly. In the purely arbitrary choice from the many which one can choose to relate, we hope we have covered this wide spectrum. The only other criterion loosely applied is to cover as wide a period as possible. While some licence may have been exercised in the individual accounts, the basic facts and events are true as recorded. The intention has been to provide an entertainment. The more serious-minded are invited to delve more deeply into historical record if they wish.

Edinburgh, 1985

CONTENTS

THE QUEEN'S SECRETARY

The death of David Rizzio, 1566

One of the most pathetic figures in Scottish history must be the daughter of James V, Mary Queen of Scots. In many respects, she was very much a victim of circumstances being somewhat ingenuous herself. She was first a woman, then sovereign. Unfortunately, she could be reasonably readily manipulated by those seeking self agrandissement but keen to have their view or ends, apparently the subject of royal approval, to lend some decency to their extremist tendencies. In no area was she used more than in the attempts to re-establish the papacy in Scotland after the Reformation which had been so recently masterminded by John Knox.

Mary had inherited the throne of Scotland on the death of her father while still only a week old. A regent was appointed, but these were troubled times and when Mary was only five years old, she was smuggled off to France to avoid capture by the English and the intrigue of the Scots. There she was to remain for the rest of her childhood, sharing the nursery of the Dauphin. At fifteen, the thrones of France and Spain recognised her as the true Queen of England as well as Scotland, and with her marriage to the Dauphin and his accession to the throne, she became Queen of France. Alas, her reign was short-lived; within two years of her marriage she was a widow. She was still only eighteen when she renounced the French court and sailed for her native land where, despite the fact that she was sovereign, few had ever seen her. For six years, she was to be the Catholic queen of a country changed out of all recognition since her expedient departure thirteen years previously.

Mary still held true to her Catholicism, it being very natural that her practice of the faith should have continued unwaveringly in one of the great bastions of the Papacy, France. It was her avowed intent that Roman Catholicism should again become the established religion of her country. On the first Sunday after her return to Scotland at the beginning of September 1561, she ordered mass to be celebrated in the Chapel Royal at Holyrood, totally oblivious to the fact that the priest could be signing his own death warrant.

Mary's closest adviser, whom many considered to have too much influence on her thoughts and actions, was her Italian secretary, David Rizzio. He had followed the ambassador from Piedmont into Scotland and first came to Mary's attention on account of his musical talents. He had been recommended to her for the bass part to complement her three valets who were often commanded to sing for her. Only a few months after her arrival, Mary appointed Rizzio a valet of her chamber. He quickly became her favourite and on the dismissal of Raulet, the secretary she had brought with her from France, Rizzio was appointed in his place. With all but his royal patron, he was unpopular from the outset. His obsequious manner and officious interference in matters of state made him the object of bitter hatred at court. He was seen as being an agent of the Pope in his duties of maintaining the Chapel Royal at Holyrood and in setting up a Roman Catholic chapel in Stirling Castle for the marriage of Mary to Henry, Lord Darnley, in July 1565. Still, the confidence he had with the queen meant that he had to be tolerated with a respect which was not too transparent. As a result of the favours bestowed on him to win his influence, Rizzio, the son of an impecunious musician in Turin, became very rich.

Although she made great play at trying to cool Darnley's approaches, it is fairly certain that Mary had fixed her affections on him long before he made any proposals of marriage. Three days before their wedding, Darnley was created Duke of Albany, however, he really looked forward to wearing the Scottish crown. It did not take long for Mary's infatuation with her handsome husband to wane as she became more aware of his weakness of character, his personal designs and his, at times, brutal disposition. She vacillated on handing over to him the supreme authority over the country.

Till now, Rizzio had been a friend of Darnley, however, his petulance and increasingly obvious failings caused the astute Rizzio's confidence in him to evaporate and he was inclined to refuse to support Darnley's pretensions to the crown matrimonial. Not only did Darnley become cold and hard towards his queen, he developed an intense hatred of her confidant whom he believed to be the chief proponent of the moves against him. He even foolishly believed that Rizzio had supplanted him in the affections of the queen; and worse, he was even inclined to the view that the child Mary was carrying was not his but that of the Italian. That the young queen could have carried such feelings for somebody who was reputedly ugly, deformed and well advanced in years, stands without any vestige of credibility. Nevertheless, Darnley nurtured intentions of murdering Rizzio to rid himself of the effects of his influence. Rizzio was not regarded in high esteem by the Protestant nobles, so Darnley did not find it difficult to find supporters for his cause who would be equally pleased to see Rizzio removed from office by whatever means might prove most efficacious. The first approach made was to Lord Ruthven who, despite his present infirmity, readily consented to engage in the murder and enrolled the active support of the Earl of Morton and Lords Lindsay and Maitland. Rizzio's murder was conceived as part of a grander plan to break up the approaching session of parliament, imprison Mary, place Darnley in the nominal sovereignty and to constitute the Earl of Moray as the head of government.

Rizzio was no one's fool and all the charades played did not prevent his being aware of the dislike with which he was generally regarded. He knew from his own country of the contempt those of rank held for those of lowly birth, regardless of their abilities. So, he tried to adopt advice given him to take a much lower profile in the politics of the country. However, Mary had grown to rely heavily on her secretary's advice and quite openly expressed the view that she considered it her prerogative as monarch to seek advice from such counsellors as she alone saw fit. Her enlightened attitude, that a man's birth did not dictate the level of his wisdom, could never be acceptable to nobles who considered that their hereditary right to rule was inviolate.

While the favour Mary showed towards Rizzio excited jealousies and envy throughout her court, her secretary was not himself unaffected. The sense of the theatrical in him caused him to begin to outvie the courtiers in the splendour of his dress. Such arrogance further incensed the court which would not readily countenance such behaviour regardless of its patronage, and thoughts of his removal were being entertained on a wider scale. Rizzio received warnings from a noted astrologer that he should tread warily but he mistook the identity of the particular person picked out for special mention in the soothsayer's advice.

Meanwhile, plans for the conspiracy against Rizzio attracted new adherents. Darnley solemnly promised his support and his defence for any involved in the deed, unaware that Maitland had already ingeniously contrived Darnley to be widely perceived as the patron of the plot. Such machinations on the part of the Protestant nobles, many of them resident south of the border, could scarcely have escaped the attention of the English monarch. In fact, Queen Elizabeth tacitly gave her approval. True to her notoriously cold-blooded nature, in spite of professions of warm feelings towards Mary, she failed to notify her of such information as she obtained. Indeed, she provided positive assistance to Lord Moray in his journey north to take part in the plot which was intended to provide for his restoration as regent.

Finally, the plot was ready for execution. On the day prior to that chosen for Rizzio's murder, Darnley challenged Rizzio to a game of tennis for the purpose of dispelling any suspicions he might have. It was suggested to Darnley that he might stab his opponent if the chance presented itself but he refused, declaring that he must be murdered in the presence of the queen in order to terrify her into acceding to the conspirators' demands. Rumours even abounded that the original plan must be followed, for Rizzio's was not the only death to be secured. It seems likely too, that some of the conspirators present at the match would have strongly disapproved of any departure since it was their intention that Rizzio should not be murdered but merely arrested and brought to trial.

It was on the evening of 9th March 1566 that the blow was struck. At dusk, about five hundred men, retainers of Morton and his accomplices, gathered in the neighbourhood of Holyrood. About seven o'clock, just over a quarter of the number were admitted to the inner courtyard by Morton who promptly issued orders for the outer gates to be locked. Meanwhile, Darnley waited in his own chambers, immediately below those of the queen, with George Douglas and Lords Ruthven and Lindsay. Upstairs, Mary was having supper with a few friends, including Rizzio, completely unsuspecting any of the sinister movements below as more of the conspirators were admitted by Darnley. Darnley climbed the private stair which led him into Mary's apartments by a concealed door in the wainscot of the room in which supper was being served. He went to sit beside Mary, put his arm round her waist and embraced her in a display of affection clearly intended for the guests' benefit. Hardly a minute had passed when Ruthven, in full armour, burst into the room from behind the concealed door followed by several of his companions. Mary was totally at a loss to explain their presence. But she was soon to be enlightened. She commanded Ruthven, his face still ghostly white with the pallor of his recent sickness, to leave immediately. He refused, indicating that no harm was intended to her, that it was David Rizzio who was the object of their interest. As he spoke, others rushed past him towards Rizzio, swords and daggers gleaming in their hands, knocking over the supper table in their haste. Kerr of Faudonside, one of the more brutally minded of the conspirators, levelled a pistol at the queen's breast, threatening that he would fire if she offered any resistance. Rizzio cowered behind Mary gripping her skirts, begging her to save him. As Darnley wrestled to break the victim's grip and to drag him in front of the

queen for her to witness his death, George Douglas snatched Darnley's dagger and buried it in Rizzio's body, over Mary's shoulder. He left the dagger with only its handle visible. Rizzio's grip loosened as his hand went to the wound. Darnley threw him to the floor and the conspirators pounced, wildly stabbing at him. Such was their uncontrolled frenzy that they not only hit the intended victim but also the other assailants. Rizzio received fifty-six wounds, thirty-four of them in the back. Darnley's dagger still remained as a symbol that he had sanctioned the murder, even if he had not actually struck a blow. Rizzio lay dead in a pool of blood which slowly spread across the floor. His body was thrown and kicked downstairs and dragged to the porter's lodge. The body was stripped of its finery and treated with every mark of indignity.

Mary and Darnley were left alone in her apartments while the assassins completed their bloody work. The full reality of the horrific scene overcame her and she fell down in a faint from which Darnley soon aroused her. Ruthven returned and poured himself a goblet of wine to wash away the taste of blood which hung around his nostrils. Mary launched a vitriolic attack on her husband who replied with equal venom and slander. A great clamour arose from downstairs, the nobles still faithful to Mary had engaged with Morton and his men in an attempt to rescue their queen. They were overcome by the force of arms and retreated to make good their escape despite Ruthven's assurances for their safety. They came to the provost of the city and apprised him of the troubles at the foot of the Canongate. A number of the burgesses marched to the palace and demanded to see the queen to be assured of her continuing safety. Darnley appeared for her, commanding them to disperse, telling them that the queen was safe and resting from her ordeal. The news that 'the Italian secretary was slain, because he had been detected in an intrigue with the Pope and the King of

Spain ... for the purpose of ... introducing Popery again into Scotland' was greeted with a cheer and the burgesses turned to make their way into the city and the various taverns to be found en route.

The queen was held captive the rest of that night. So great was her agitation and terror, for she feared that Ruthven was intent on murdering her too, that she was in danger of suffering a miscarriage. But still, ill as she was, she planned to avenge her secretary's death. In due course, rigorous prosecutions were instituted against the assassins. But, with the exception of Ruthven (who died three months later), Kerr of Faudonside and George Douglas, all were received back into royal favour before the end of the year. Only four people were convicted of charges arising out of the affair. Thomas Scott of Cambusmichael (then Sheriff-Depute of Perth), William Harlaw and John Mowbray were charged with treasonably holding the queen in captivity, while carrying arms, within her chambers, after the murder of Rizzio. Henry Yair, formerly a priest connected with the Chapel Royal, was charged with assisting the conspirators and concealing information of their treasonable conspiracy. Harlaw and Mowbray were pardoned on the intercession of the Earl of Bothwell. However, Scott and Yair were sentenced to be hung, drawn and quartered. Scott's head was stuck on a spike on one of the towers of the palace, while Yair's was spiked at the Netherbow.

The day after his murder, Rizzio's body was obscurely buried in the Canongate churchyard though it was subsequently exhumed and re-interred in the grounds of Holyrood Chapel. To this day, there is a dark, irregular stain on the floor outside the door to Mary's apartments which, it is asserted, is due to Rizzio's blood.

THE LAIRD O' WARRISTON

The murder of John Kincaid, 1600

Few cases of murder can have excited such lively interest in the public mind at the time of their occurrence as that of John Kincaid, Laird of Warriston, in July 1600. It was an event which was commemorated in at least three ballads which were still being sung well into the nineteenth century. Unfortunately, these three versions each had slightly differing accounts of the murder which makes reconstruction of the true story difficult without recourse to contemporary reports of the trial and condemnation of the culprits, none of which is necessarily a full account. Nevertheless, the speculation and supposition do not in any way detract from the essentials of the story.

In the sixteenth and into the seventeenth centuries, Warriston House commanded an open position with splendid views towards the Forth and southwards to the old city. During this period, it was in the possession of the Kincaid family who then also owned extensive estates across central Scotland. John Kincaid, the proprietor, lived there with his wife, Jean Livingstone, the young and beautiful daughter of Lord Dunipace. It is generally believed that the laird was considerably older than his wife and that while he married for love, her reasons were rather more mercenary. The marriage was unhappy though it is uncertain whether their notoriously unfriendly relations were caused by the disparity in years or the alleged brutality of the laird. It is to be assumed

Warriston House

that the faults were not solely one sided. In due course, Lady Warriston resolved to rid herself of her husband on a very flimsy pretext which propriety caused to be advanced in preference to the true reasons. However, she had to find some way of achieving her purpose, unaccustomed as she was to the darker aspects of Edinburgh's society.

Among the staff employed in the household was Janet Murdo, described as Lady Warriston's nurse. Jean would frequently confide her unhappiness to her nurse, and naturally, it was to her that she first went looking for assistance. By strange coincidence, Janet Murdo was particularly friendly with Robert Weir, a stable-lad employed by her mistress' father. She implied that he might possibly be of help. She undertook to approach him with regard to the matter and, should he be unwilling, she would seek another. Failing that, she was even prepared to commit the act herself, being fully in accord with Jean's purpose.

Weir showed that he did not fear the challenge and was no doubt attracted by the prospects for supplementing his meagre income. On two or three occasions, he came to

Warriston ostensibly to see Janet Murdo, but in fact to discuss the matter of the laird's murder. However, it was not until 1st July, at least a month after he was first approached, that an interview could take place with Lady Warriston. It was decided that the deed be done that night. He was secretly taken down into one of the cellars of the house to await darkness.

In the early hours of 2nd July, Jean Livingstone made her way to Weir's hiding place and led him from the cellar, through the entrance hall and silently up the wide staircase to her husband's bed-chamber. They entered the room but the noise roused John Kincaid from his light sleep and he started to rise. Jean Livingstone immediately withdrew but Weir flew at Kincaid, delivering him a kick in the side of the neck, knocking him from his bed to the floor. Kincaid cried out in pain. Fearing that the noise had been heard by the household, according to the indictment at Weir's trial, 'he thaireftir maist tyrannouslie and barbarouslie with his hand grippit him be the thrott . . . which he held fast ane long tyme till he wirreit [strangled] him; during the which tyme the said Johnne Kincaid lay struggilling and fechting in the panes of daith under him. And . . . Johnne was crewallie murdreist and slain be the said Robert.' It is interesting that the method actually employed by Weir was the same as that used more than two centuries later by the infamous pair Burke and Hare when conducting their evil traffic in bodies for the anatomist.

The indictment of Weir inferred that Lady Warriston was present, or close by, at the time of the death, but makes no mention of the active participation of Janet Murdo or any other accomplice. In fact, Lady Warriston herself played a very passive part in the actual commissioning of the crime. According to her confession given to her spiritual adviser (which he included in a memorial to support the sincerity of her contrition)—'I think I hear presently the pitifull and fearfull cryes which he gave when he was strangled! And that sin which I committed, in murdering mine own husband, is yet before me. When that horrible and fearfull sin was done, I desyred the unhappy man who did it, for my own part, the Lord knoweth I laid never my hands upon him to do evil; but as soon as that man gripped him and began his evil turn, so soon as my husband cryed so fearfully, I leapt out over my bed, and went to the Hall; where I sat all the time, till that unhappy man came to me and reported that mine husband was dead.' She implored Weir to take her away with him, for she feared the ignominy of being brought to trial and the disgrace it would bring on her family. However, Weir argued that if she were to disappear, then that would be implicit of her guilt. However, if he were to flee alone, the guilt would be perceived as his alone. It is open to conjecture the sincerity of his gallant words. At any rate, he left alone leaving Jean Livingstone and Janet Murdo in the house.

The next morning, the officers of justice arrived at Warriston House. It is not at all clear how they had gained any suspicion that a crime had been committed. They found the laird's body and immediately apprehended Lady Warriston and her nurse along with two domestic servants accused of being 'hyred women'. All four were placed under custody in the Tolbooth. News of the arrest reached Weir who promptly absconded from his position at Holyrood.

The four women were adjudged to have been taken 'red-hand' and accordingly, they were taken before the Magistrates of Edinburgh on Thursday, 3rd July, the third day after the murder. Unfortunately, the trial records no longer exist, so it is impossible to give much detail of the events transpiring. Although we do know that Lady Warriston did not plead guilty, it is not known whether she was indicted as the principal defendant or merely as art and part in the crime. Equally, the evidence led remains a mystery. Weir, the actual murderer, had,

18

for the time being, disappeared, the nurse clearly was not the type to turn informer and she, along with one of the 'hyred women', was ultimately convicted. The other servant appears not to have been brought to trial, which may have been her consideration for turning King's evidence. It is supposed that she may well have been convinced by the strong arguments put forward by 'the Boot'. This was one of the plethora of instruments of torture in common use at the time. It consisted of two wooden shells which, when placed together, had the shape of a boot. The device was strapped to the unfortunate victim's leg so that it encased the leg to just above the knee. A wedge was then placed between the knee-cap and the top lip of the boot. This would then be driven downwards with the aid of the mallet. The prosecutor seldom failed to obtain the required testimony.

Lady Warriston spoke selflessly on behalf of her co-defendants: 'As to these weemen who was challenged with me, I will also tell you my minde concerning them. God forgive the nurse, for she helped me too well in mine evill purpose; . . . As for the other weeman, I request that you neither put them to death, nor any torture; because I testify they are both innocent; and knew nothing of this deed before it was done, and the mean time of doing it.' However, her pleadings were to little avail. While she was found guilty and condemned to die as she had more or less begged the court to do, the other two on trial with her were treated equally with her. The usual punishment for such a crime as hers was handed down—burning after being strangled at the stake (on occasion, courts were not unknown to decide the criminal be burnt alive). However, owing to her rank and the intercession of her influential friends, this was subsequently mitigated to decapitation by 'the Maiden'— the Scottish equivalent of the guillotine.

In the interval between sentence and its execution, the young Lady Warriston, still only twenty-one years old, was subjected to the interminable attentions of a minister anxious to bring repentance into her heart before she went into her Maker's presence. According to a pamphlet published soon after her death, he was entirely successful. She was converted from a state of callous indifference to one of lively sensibility and religious harmony, regarding her approaching death as a just expiation of her offence. Still, her family were unimpressed by her contrition. None of them visited her in prison. Indeed, so deeply did they resent the disgrace she had brought upon them that not only did they do nothing to intervene on her behalf but they even tried to have her execution brought forward in order that the continuing publicity of their position be brought to a swift end. Their petitions were overruled.

At three o'clock on the morning of Saturday 5th July, the Magistrates arrived at the prison to accompany her to her place of execution at the Girth Cross, the ancient boundary of the Abbey Sanctuary at the foot of the Canongate. The uncommonly early hour appeared to be the only concession to the family's pleas. When they came to the scaffold, she openly made her confession to those assembled:

'The occasion of my coming here, is to shew that I am, and have been a great sinner, and hath offended the Lord's Majesty; especially, of the cruell murdering of mine own husband; which, albeit I did not with mine own hands, for I never laid mine hands upon him all the time that he was murdering; yet I was the diviser of it, and so the committer! But my God hath been alwise mercifull to me, and hath given me repentance for my sins; and I hope for mercy and grace at his Majesty's hands, for his dear son Jesus Christ's sake.' Jean Livingstone's conduct on the scaffold was exemplary. After her devotional exercises, she handed over a clean piece of linen and a pin to bind it round her face. The minister who had virtually been her constant companion throughout the previous thirty-six hours could no longer control his emotions. He left her side before breaking down in tears. She knelt down before the block and offered her neck. The executioner made her head fast and pulled back her feet in order that her neck would be stretched out longer. The axe was raised to its fullest extent. Lady Warriston continued her prayers: 'O, lamb of God, that taketh away the sins of the world, have mercy on me! Into my hands, O Lord . . .' The axe fell.

Though it was just four o'clock in the morning, a large crowd had gathered to witness the execution. Despite the fact that the other two women sentenced to die did so according to the usual method, strangling and burning, at the same early hour at the Castlehill, the Warristons' hopes that this would be a more attractive spectacle were not fulfilled. They had not reckoned with the human foible of extracting delight from seeing those of high station humbled to the level of the ordinary man.

But what of Robert Weir? It was not for another four years until he was brought to justice. He was put up for trial at the High Court of Justiciary on 26th June 1604. The prosecution on the indictment was conducted by the three brothers of the murdered laird. The case was so clear that no witnesses were called and the verdict of guilty returned by the jury was merely a formality. James Sterling then pronounced sentence:

'Descernit and ordanit the said Robert Weir to be tane to ane scaffold to be fixt besyde the Croce of Edinburgh, and thair to be brokin upoune ane [wheel] till he be deid, and to ly thairat during the space of [twenty-four] hours. And thaireftir his body to be tane upon the said [wheel] and set up in ane publict place betwixt the place of Warestoun and the toun of Leyth; and to remane thairupoune ay and till command be gevin for the buriall thairoff.' Very rarely was such a horrible form of

21

execution decreed. Never known in England, but relatively common in France and Germany, tying the convict to a cart-wheel and driving at speed through the streets was apparently adopted when it was felt that the atrocity of the crime should be impressed upon the public. In Weir's case, the unprovoked and barbarous murder of the nobleman by a servant was considered well worthy of an agonising and lingering death.

The "Maiden"
(From the Instrument in the possession of the Society of Antiquaries of Scotland)

HELL HATH NO FURY!

The murder of Lord Forrester, 1679

In medieval times, Edinburgh was entirely built round the ridge running eastwards from the castle. It consisted of little more than what now constitutes the High Street with a series of closes and wynds running at right angles off it. It was the custom to name these after the owners of the property situated in them. Thus, considerable confusion could arise as owners changed and closes gained new names. Fortunately, the names of many of them did stay relatively fixed for long periods and helped to provide a certain stabilising influence to help the citizens maintain some orientation datum. One of these was Forrester's Close which was on the south side of the ridge close to St Giles Church. Here was to be found the house of Adam Forrester.

Little is known of his early life, but Adam Forrester made quite an impression from the time he first appeared in public life on appointment as Justice Clerk in 1362. He quickly rose to become provost of Edinburgh in 1373 and, soon afterwards, Deputy Governor of Edinburgh Castle. He was a very successful merchant, amassing a sizeable fortune in the reign of David II, largely through trade with England. In 1376, he was confirmed as the owner of the lands of Corstorphine, old estates then located far outside the city boundaries, having bought them from the Mores of Abercorne. Thus began a long association between the Forrester family and the developing community and village which was to make the names of Forrester and Corstorphine virtually synonymous, until the estates were bought over by Sir James Dick of Prestonfield in 1713.

Title to Adam Forrester's lands progressed through the direct male line for eight generations down to George Forrester. He was a man of talent and probity, held high in favour with Charles I who created him first Lord Forrester of Corstorphine in 1633. He had four daughters by his wife Christian, but no male heir. Two of his daughters were married to sons of Lieutenant General William Baillie, a man who had made a name for himself in the Covenanting Wars—Joanna to James Baillie and Lilias to William Baillie. His other daughters, Helen and Christian, were married to Lord Ross of Hawkhead and James Hamilton of Grange respectively. Presented with the problem of who should succeed to his land and titles on his death, George Forrester obtained a new patent from the King providing to himself in life-rent, and after his decease, 'to, or in favour of, his daughter Joanna and her husband James Baillie and the heirs procreate betwixt them; whom failing, to the nearest lawful heir-male of the said James whatever, they carrying the name and arms of Forrester.' The patent was granted in 1650, a matter of weeks before the battle of Worcester, and George Forrester died soon afterwards. James Baillie took on his father-in-law's name to become the second Lord Forrester.

Despite the fact that the new Lord Forrester was a zealous Presbyterian who was said to have supported the building of a special meeting-house in Corstorphine, his strict religious principles did not prevent him enjoying female company. It is said that his activities in this direction caused his wife such grief that she was driven to an early grave. He subsequently married the daughter of the famous Cavalier general, Patrick Ruthven, Earl of Forth and Brentford, by whom he had three sons and two daughters, all of whom assumed the name, Ruthven. The second Lord Forrester was an ardent royalist and was actively engaged with the party during the time of the Commonwealth. As a result of a proclamation he issued calling on all persons residing in Midlothian to put forth horse according to their rents for the King's army, he was fined £2,500 sterling and his estate was overrun and destroyed by the English troops. As a consequence of these proceedings, his financial affairs became very involved, and, being unable to pay the provisions left to his mother and his sisters and to meet the oustanding debts of the first Lord Forrester, the rents of his estates were assigned to numerous creditors. He became dissipated and abandoned in his character, and turned to the consolations provided by drink. He also formed a stormy and dangerous relationship with a rather attractive woman called Christian Nimmo, the wife of a rich Edinburgh merchant. Mrs Nimmo had a rather more violent and impulsive character than her innocent good looks would have suggested. She was even said to commonly carry a concealed weapon. It was claimed that she was related to a Mrs Bedford, a remarkably wicked adulteress who had murdered her husband and to Lady Warriston who had been beheaded for the same crime in 1600. She was not a woman to be treated lightly.

Rumours ran round the village and in the city for many years but their relationship remained intact until further information on Mrs Nimmo's ancestry was discovered and revealed. Her maiden name was Christian Hamilton, daughter of Christian and James Hamilton. She was thus the niece of Lord Forrester's first wife, Joanna, and a grand-daughter of the first Lord Forrester. The scandal caused James Forrester to unilaterally terminate their mutual acquaintance; however, Christian Nimmo was not going to accept being summarily dismissed as if she were just a servant girl. Lord Forrester was incensed by the fact that his lover must have been fully aware of their kinship but had never told him. One evening, when drunk, he slandered her at length with the foulest of accusations. Unfortunately for him, reports of this reached Christian's ears.

Feelings still ran high when on the evening of 26th August 1679, Christian Nimmo set out for the Forresters' residence, Corstorphine Castle, attended by her maid. When they arrived, they were told that Lord Forrester was at the Black Bull Inn, one of his customary haunts, which was sited in the main street of the village opposite the parish church. She despatched her maid to fetch him to her. She paced about the grounds of the castle, her wrath increasing the longer he kept her waiting. Eventually, Forrester arrived and met up with Mrs Nimmo close to a large sycamore tree near the old dovecot. A bitter argument developed. In his drunken state, Lord Forrester's reactions were too slow for him to prevent his sword being snatched from his side. Inspired by her fury, Christian Nimmo, standing in front of him, ran the sword through his vitals with such force that its tip pierced the skin of his back close to his spine. Her victim sank to his knees, coughing up blood, disbelief in his eyes. He breathed his last, fell forward on to the sword. The blade completed its passage through his body. Christian Nimmo casually walked away and back to the castle. Her thirst for revenge satiated, her fury dropped from her and she came to a sudden realisation of her crime. She hid in a garrett in the castle but she was discovered by one of her slippers which had dropped through a crevice of the floor. She was seized and brought before the Sheriffs of Edinburgh to whom she confessed her crime but sought to extenuate it by claiming that Lord Forrester, intoxicated and furious at the bitterness she had shown in their argument, had drawn his sword and ran at her. She said that she had taken the sword from him, for her own protection, and that he had fallen upon it.

Christian Nimmo's trial was held two days later. Her guilt was deemed proven and she was condemned to die.

She was sent to the Tolbooth to wait the appointed time. However, playing on the humanity the law can at times display, she obtained a two months stay of execution by deceiving the court into believing that she was pregnant. Despite the care with which she was guarded, on 29th September, she managed to escape from the Tolbooth dressed as a man, in clothes smuggled in to her by friends. Her freedom was short-lived. She was recaptured at Fala Mill the next day by the Ruthven sons of Lord Forrester. On 12th November, 1679, wearing a 'whyte taffetie hood' and dress, she was led out to be beheaded at the Market Cross where she is said to have bared her neck and shoulders to the executioner with the utmost courage.

The crime had an interesting sequel characteristic of the age in which it took place. Lord Forrester left heirs only of his second marriage who were in possession of the family honours and estates which had come to him by his first wife. They had taken the name of Ruthven, whereas, it will be recalled, the patent obtained by the 1st Lord Forrester ordained that the inheritors must carry the Forrester name. Lilias Forrester and her son, William Baillie of Torwoodhead, feared that the Ruthvens might interfere with the late Lord's charter-chest and so prejudice their rights to succession. So, with the help of several friends they forced their way into the castle while the murder victim's body still lay there, unburied. On a complaint from the Ruthvens, the intruders were brought before the Lords of Council. Despite protesting that their only aim was to ensure that no documents were embezzled or destroyed, their Lordships adjudged that Baillie and his mother be detained in prison at their pleasure. At the same time, the court took charge of the charter-chest. In due course, William Baillie's claim was upheld and he became the third Lord Forrester of Corstorphine.

The same sycamore under whose branches the murder was committed still stands, protected by a preservation order. Legends have grown up of a woman, dressed in white and carrying a bloody sword, being seen walking between the sycamore and the dovecot. That the dovecot still stands testifies to the strength of the superstition that its destruction would be followed within a year by the death of the lady of the house in whose grounds it is to be found.

Tomb of the Forresters, Corstorphine Church

'THE PERFIDIOUS APOSTATE'

The assassination of Archbishop James Sharp, 1679

In complete contrast to its true ideals, religion, regardless of its particular deity or method of worship, has been the root cause of disquiet, unrest, insurrection and war throughout history in every country with any significant history. This is no less true in Scotland where events of the 16th and 17th centuries were pervaded at every turn by the battles between the Roman church and the non-conformists and the internecine strife between the supporters of the different forms of church government within the non-conformist ranks. The Scots reformers were very much influenced by John Knox and the presbyterian precepts he learned from Calvin. However, the Stuart dynasty had leanings towards episcopacy, since this presented the monarchy with the opportunity to control church government by way of its patronage of the appointment of the bishops. Presbyterianism and its own self government was too democratic. One of the principle targets of the popular hatred to emerge during the period when episcopacy was the official religion despite the affirmations and intents enshrined in the National Covenant, was James Sharp, Archbishop of St Andrews.

Sharp pursued his religious studies at Aberdeen where episcopacy was favoured. Thus, at the time he sought a charge, he was forced to go south of the border. However, before he could make any significant progress in the Church of England, he fell ill and was advised that he should return to Scotland. He found a position at the University of St Andrews. In due course, he became minister at Crail. By this time, there were no bishops in Scotland and so he had to preach as a presbyterian, though privately he still held to his episcopalian principles.

With the restoration of Charles I, came the resolve to restore the prelacy to Scotland. The presbyterians were fully aware of the dangers to their liberties and deputed Sharp to put their case. He was considered to be a man of much ability and learning, of plausible manners and of singular dexterity in the management of men. He had somehow acquired the complete confidence of his party. For a time, he was able to zealously promote their views in London and even procured the King's written affirmation 'to preserve and protect the government of the Church of Scotland, as settled by law, without violation.' However, he was shrewd enough to realise that these were empty promises and that the restoration of the prelacy in Scotland was inevitable. He was secretly gained over by some of the English high church statesmen and caused to betray the church whose cause he was supposed to be advocating. His skills were put to the test when he returned to Scotland and had to conceal his perfidy. They were fully equal to the task.

In spite of his oath to preserve the presbyterian system, Charles issued a proclamation in 1661 announcing the restoration of the prelacy, prohibiting all meetings called in protest at the change and enjoining all burghs not to appoint any to office who held presbyterian principles. Episcopacy was now the established religion and one of the four suffragan bishops appointed to take charge of ecclesiastical affairs was James Sharp, as primate and archbishop of St Andrews. His true colours were now revealed. He immediately entered into the persecution of the covenanters and earned for himself the deep and bitter hatred of his fellow countrymen. His apostasy and perfidy brought him universal odium and the increasing vigour with which he pursued those who sought to embrace presbyterianism made it inevitable that an attempt should be made on his life.

James Mitchell was educated at Edinburgh University where he bound himself to the provisions of the National Covenant. Soon after the Pentland uprising, at which he had not actually been present, he went to Flanders returning to Scotland some months later to find that his name was not included amongst those to whom mercy or favour had been extended in the aftermath of the uprising. Technically, he had still not laid down his arms. He was continually harassed by his fears of being taken, and adopted the resolution of avenging the wrongs done to himself and to the nation by despatching the man he saw as the main instigator of the oppression and bloodshed, James Sharp.

On the afternoon of 11th July, 1668, he waited at the head of Blackfriar's Wynd to meet Archbishop Sharp's coach outside the primate's house. The coach arrived to collect the archbishop and Honeyman, the Bishop of Orkney, and as soon as Sharp had taken his seat, Mitchell stepped out and levelled a pistol at him. Just as Honeyman reached up his hand to step into the coach, Mitchell discharged the pistol. Honeyman received the full force of the shot in the wrist and arm. Sharp survived the assassination attempt without injury. Mitchell hurried quickly away to Niddry's Wynd and into his lodgings in Stevenlaw's Close where he changed his clothes. He came straight back into the street as being the place where he would be least expected. The cry went up that a man had been killed; but when it was made known that it was only a bishop, all was calmed and no attempts made to find and arrest the would-be assassin.

Two days later, the Privy Council issued a proclamation offering a substantial reward to anyone giving information that would help discover the perpetrator, with a pardon to be granted to any of his accessories. It was to no avail. The foolhardy and criminal attempt was entirely Mitchell's own plan, so there was none who could provide information. The attempt was at first followed by increased severities against the presbyterians who, without the slightest evidence, were accused of having a hand in the design. Sharp, on the other hand, seems to have been convinced that it might be more sensible to be less oppressive and so he began to show less opposition to the proposals for offering indulgences to a certain number of the presbyterian ministers who had been ejected from their churches.

Six years had passed by when Sharp's attention was drawn to the features of a man who kept a small shop in the High Street near to his residence and who appeared to watch him with a sinister eye each time he passed. The more he examined the man, the more clearly did he recall the face of the man who had tried to shoot him. He arranged for his brother, with a number of servants, to seize the man and to deliver him to the custody of the Privy Council. Mitchell was reported to be in possession of two loaded pistols when taken.

On 10th February, 1647, Mitchell was brought before a committee of the Council. With no proof against him, and having been seized without warrant, it was obvious that evidence would need to be manufactured or a confession would need to be extorted from the accused before a charge could be brought or be sustained at trial. Mitchell knew with whom he was dealing in Sharp and resolutely refused to make any acknowledgment of guilt unless he received an official assurance of pardon. Such a course he knew would be anathema to his principal accuser and was calculated to cause the greatest ire. He had visions of being a martyr and ensuring that others would make doubly sure of succeeding where he had failed. The Lord Chancellor took him aside and swore on his own oath and reputation as Chancellor that he would save his life if Mitchell confessed. His private intervention bore fruit. As the minutes of the full Council for 12th March record: 'All having retired, apart with one of the said committee, he did then confess, upon his knees, he was the person—upon assurance given him by one of the committee as to his lyfe, who had warrand from the lord-commissioner and council to give the same—and did thereafter freely confess before all the lords that were on the said committee, that he shott the said pistoll at the said archbishop, and did subscrybe his confession in presence of the said committee, which is also subscrybed by them.'

Mitchell was remitted to the Justice Court to receive his indictment, and the Council, after deliberation on the punishment which should accompany the conviction, decided that his sentence should be to have his right hand struck off at the Cross of Edinburgh. He duly appeared before the Lords of Justiciary on 2nd March. As he passed the bench, one of the judges, who was generally believed to hate Sharp, said to him, 'Confess nothing, unless you are sure of your limbs as well as your life.' Whether as a direct consequence of this advice or not, Mitchell refused to repeat his confession before the Court and insisted that the allegations of the indictment against him be proved. The prosecution had no evidence other than the confession and for this to be available to secure conviction it had to be repeated in court. The court could not recognise extra judicial confession of a pannel against himself. The Lords on the bench postponed the matter till the 25th. Meanwhile the Council made an Act rescinding any promises made in its name and decreeing that the law must take its course. The hand of Sharp could be seen operating behind the scenes having now mounted a personal vendetta against Mitchell. On appearance back at court, it was still uncertain what was to be done and Mitchell was remanded in prison. He languished on the Bass Rock for two years.

Early on the evening of 18th January, 1676, Mitchell was brought before the Privy Council to be examined by torture. He was asked whether he would adhere to his former confession. He refused. He was called again four days later and again two days after that. Each time he remained obdurate. On his last appearance, the president drew his attention to the 'boots' lying on the table before him. Mitchell still refused to accede to the Council's demand and so the executioner was commanded to strap on the evil instrument of torture before the Council and the Lords of Justiciary, whose presence had been commanded. The wedges were put in place in front of his knee cap. The executioner began to drive them in, after each stroke the prisoner being asked if he had anything to say. After the ninth stroke, he fainted through the pain, but without a confession of guilt. The torture was stopped and Mitchell was returned to his imprisonment.

He was at length brought to trial in January, 1678, at the instigation of Sharp, for the offence committed ten years previously. On the 3rd of the month the eloquent and skilful Sir George Lockhart and Mr John Ellis were appointed as counsel for Mitchell. But Sharp would have his life and he set out to suborn the witnesses to Mitchell's confession. As a result, Lords Rothes, Hatton and Lauderdale as well as Sharp himself appeared as witnesses for the prosecution. Under cross-examination, each solemnly denied under oath that any assurance of life had been given the accused. Lockhart would now produce his trump card. From amongst his papers, he produced and started to read a copy of the act of the Privy Council containing the promise of pardon. He demanded that the original record should be laid before the court. After much debate, he was overruled on the basis that the records contained state secrets which should not be laid before open court. Under normal circumstances, Lockhart's arguments would have been enough to see his client acquitted. But, even the jury was stacked against him. All its members, in the pay of the government, returned a verdict of guilty. The prisoner heard the sentence of death pronounced.

The Lords who stood accused of perjuring themselves repaired to the Council chamber to consult the records. The evidence was unequivocal. Each was inclined towards granting a respite towards the prisoner, without actually making any statement prejudicing their own integrity. The primate would have none of it. He insisted on the sentence being carried out as a way of securing his own life against the repetition of further attempts. Mitchell was undoubtedly a dangerous fanatic whose crime, if proved, deserved punishment. However, his fault is lost sight of in the complicated intrigue of perjury, cruelty and treachery shown by members of the establishment.

Though Sharp hoped to ensure his own longevity, his contrived murder of Mitchell did not go long without retribution. He was to meet his God before Mitchell met his. Unlike Mitchell's unsuccessful attempt on Sharp, the successful assassins' intentions had long been premeditated, though the ultimate execution owed more to fortuity than any would have envisaged or felt desirable.

One of the primate's chief agents in the north of Fife was a man by the name of Carmichael. His cruel tortures on wives, children and servants of the covenanters were so barbarous that a dozen small proprietors of the area resolved to inflict exemplary punishment on him. They also harboured the desire of reaching Sharp himself since Carmichael's actions were ultimately carried out in his name and so were his responsibility. On 3rd May, 1679, this band, led by David Hackston of Rathillet and John Balfour of Burley, lay in wait for Carmichael near Struthers, in north east Fife. Unfortunately, their target was forewarned and managed to escape. They were about to go their separate ways again and wait for another

occasion when the young son of a local farmer ran up to tell them that Archbishop Sharp had been seen approaching St Andrews on his journey from Edinburgh. They could not believe their good fortune, but immediately interpreted it as a divine call to them to execute justice against their arch-persecutor. The band made chase and caught sight of the archbishop's coach on Magus Muir, about three miles from its destination. Looking round, the coachman saw the conspirators riding behind at full speed, pistols and swords drawn. He ordered the postillion to drive on at increased speed. Wondering why his coach was travelling at uncustomary pace, Sharp looked out the coach window, only to quickly draw his head back in as a pistol was fired at him. Within half a mile, the pursuers overtook the coach and, cutting the traces, brought it to a halt. A shot was fired in through the window and wounded Sharp, the ball lodged just below the collar bone. The coach door was pulled open and the primate and his daughter, with whom he was travelling, were ordered out. His protestations earned him a sword near the kidneys. Hands reached into the coach and dragged the occupants out to the ground. Sharp poured out entreaties for his life, promising indemnities and money. He even offered to renounce his office. But the conspirators were steeled against his supplications with passion even stronger than revenge. They reminded him of his empty promises to Mitchell. All the while, they taunted and struck him with their swords. The blood stains on his robes spread wider. The primate recognised one of his attackers, Balfour, and on his knees, beseeched him, as a gentleman, to spare his life. He reached out his hand, but a sword flashed through the air and half severed his hand from the wrist. He fell forward in pain, his forehead on the ground. The conspirators cut and hacked at the back of his head till it was gashed into a large bloody hole. To make sure of his death a sword tip was pushed into the hole and his brain stirred inside the skull. Miss Sharp's prayers and attempts to save her father were to no avail. She herself received many wounds as she came between each murderous sword and her father.

The deed done, the band ransacked the coach, leaving its occupants to make their own way to find help. So effective was their escape, and the support of the community for their action that despite intensive efforts on the part of the authorities, Hackston and his band were never brought to book. Records of the prisoners held in the Tolbooth in Edinburgh show the names of various men detained for participating in the murder of Sharp. Not one of them was a member of the band responsible and all were liberated.

In modern times, it is claimed that a ghostly coach can still occasionally be seen on the road towards St Andrews from Magus Muir. Whether it is Sharp's coach or not, no one is particularly anxious to find out for sure, for its sighting is a portent of a death in the family within the week.

———————

TRIAL BY TOUCH

The case of Philip Stanfield, 1687

Although the murder of Sir James Stanfield took place at
New Mills near Haddington, rather than in Edinburgh,
the fact of its proximity to the capital, the trial being held
in Edinburgh and certain intriguing and unique aspects
surrounding the murder and subsequent trial provide
justification enough for including it in this collection. Up
to the beginning of this century, it was still one of only
four parricides recorded in Scottish criminal annals and it
was the last case of an accused being convicted on the
ancient ordeal of the Law of the Bier.

James Stanfield, a Yorkshireman by birth, was a
colonel in the ranks of the Parliamentary forces in the
English Civil War. After Cromwell's victory at the Battle
of Dunbar, he was one of those enterprising Englishmen
who could see business opportunities in Scotland for
those willing to stay. Accordingly, he purchased land on
the banks of the Tyne near Haddington and there re-
established a cloth manufacturing business abandoned
thirty years earlier. He enjoyed the patronage of the
Protector, Oliver Cromwell, and after the Restoration,
having declared his fealty to the crown, had many
privileges conferred on him by Charles II, including a
knighthood.

In 1681, as part of the general effort to develop
indigenous industries which could compete with those
south of the border and help redress the imbalance in
trade between the two countries, Stanfield became one of
those very much involved in the plans for his adopted

country, the success of his mills at Haddington making him well qualified to advise on the cloth industry and to oversee ambitious development plans. Sir James' business ability made him a wealthy man but he was considerably less successful in his private life. His wife showed little interest in, and provided less support for, his ventures while the profligacy of his elder son, Philip, was a source of considerable anguish.

Philip was, according to the indictment finally brought against him, a 'debauched person [who] did committ and was accessory to several notorious villainies both at home and abroad.' Little is known of his earlier life. He was at one time a student at St Andrews University where he incurred the wrath of John Knox's great grandson, John Welsh, by hitting him with a hymn-book during his sermon. He subsequently entered the Scots Regiment but seemed to spend more time in prison or confined to barracks than in action. At one stage, he even languished in the condemned cell but managed to effect his escape. His father would continually bail him out of his difficulties, but far from showing any gratitude, the son would abuse and curse his unfortunate father. On two occasions, he actually made attempts on his life. On the first, he 'did chase and pursue his father upon the King's highway at Lothian-burn, and did fire pistols upon him' and again made a similar attempt at Culterallors.

In due course, much of Sir James' fortune evaporated and his financial embarrassment caused him to set in train the sale to his company of his personal holdings in the buildings and land on which the cloth manufactory was sited. Meanwhile, he decided to disinherit Philip in favour of his second son, John. However, John was only a little better than Philip in the extent of his excesses. It is hardly surprising that Sir James exhibited bouts of melancholy. Philip tried to attribute this to a mental derangement. But, fortunately, physicians could easily put the lie to this. Despite the worries which hung heavy on him, his reason and mental capacity remained unimpaired.

Matters finally came to a head in November, 1687. On the last Saturday of the month, Sir James made his customary trip into Edinburgh on business. On his return, he dined with a long-time friend who was to preach in the local pulpit the next morning. The two men were relaxed and enjoyed each other's company until shortly after ten o'clock, when, tired by the rigours of their ride from the capital, they retired to their rooms. Sir James' friend, John Bell, slept but fitfully. During the night, he was awakened by an anguished cry and for a time afterwards, heard a great confusion of noise and voices. They appeared to be outside his door and on the stairs, and at times in the room below. He discreetly locked his door more securely, concerned for his own safety, for he knew that some of his recent treatises on witchcraft had caused disquiet in the land and threats of personal injury had been directed at him. He next heard the voices outside the house and went to the window but found himself unable to open it to discern what caused the commotion. The voices gradually moved away down the garden towards the river and peace returned.

Next morning, Sir James was found to be missing from his room. A search was begun and before long his body was found floating face downwards in an icy pool in the river bordering the grounds of his house. He was carried up to the house by his servants but Philip would not let the body in 'for he had not died like a man but like a beast.' Accordingly, the body was deposited in an outhouse. Philip asserted that his father had taken his own life—a view, at first, shared generally. However, the minister took a very different stance bearing in mind his experience of the previous night. He thought it desirable to have the body examined by a physician, being inclined to the view that Sir James may have been murdered.

Rumour grew through the early morning on how Sir James had met his end and at the instigation of his mill manager, Umphray Spurway, the Lord Advocate ordered that the body be viewed to determine whether foul play might be suspected. However, when the messenger carrying this order came to New Mills, he was intercepted by Philip who suppressed the letter.

Around three o'clock in the morning, Spurway was awakened and, looking out of his window, saw horses and several torches around the gate of the main house. He went to investigate only to be told that Philip was attending to the burial of his father, having received orders from the Lord Advocate to that effect. He refused to join the cortege to the small churchyard three miles distant, where a grave was hastily dug in the frosty ground. The next morning, he organised representations to the legal authorities in Edinburgh regarding the burial and as a result, the next night, he was again aroused from his bed. This time he found five men at his door, two being Edinburgh surgeons and a third, James Row, a relative of Sir James. They carried with them an order from the Lord Advocate for the exhumation of Sir James Stanfield's body. They immediately went to the churchyard, collecting Philip Stanfield on the way. The body was disinterred and carried into the church for examination. The surgeons made an incision near the neck and it became quite obvious to them that Sir James had been strangled. Suicide was immediately dismissed.

When the autopsy was completed, the surgeons asked for help in replacing the body in the coffin. In the subsequent trial, it became apparent that the whole procedure had been deliberately set up to subject Philip to the ordeal by touch. According to custom, Philip lifted his father's head. No sooner had he done so than blood was seen to rush from the surgeons' incision, despite the fact that they had carefully sewn it up and cleaned the body. Philip dropped the head in horror, '—and fled from

42

the body! —And, in consternation and confusion, cryed, "Lord, have mercy upon me!" —and bowed himself down over a seat in the church, wiping his father's innocent blood off his own murdering hands, upon his cloaths!' He utterly refused to touch the body again. The incident was accepted in accordance with the writings of King James that 'if the dead carkasse be at any time thereafter handled by the murtheror, it will gushe out of blood, as if the blood were crying to heaven for revenge of the murtheror.'

Philip Stanfield was arrested and brought to stand trial before the High Court of Justiciary in Edinburgh on the 6th February, 1688, on an indictment which by today's standards would appear inordinately long. He faced three charges—high treason, as having drunk a toast of confusion to the King; cursing his father; and murder of his father. Each was punishable by death.

Initial submissions by the defence regarded the relevancy of the charges, but they were dismissed and a jury was empanelled to hear the case. The first two charges were easily proven. The main content of the proceedings was concerned with the death of Sir James.

The medical report established the cause of death as being strangulation, bruising round the neck, the bruised blood inside the incision, the dislocation of the neck and the total lack of water inside the body being the confirmatory evidence. Several witnesses swore to the animosity which Philip frequently demonstrated towards his father. It further appeared that he had, on several occasions immediately prior to his father's death, boasted that he would be laird before Christmas. Philip's mother herself was not completely free from suspicion of being an accessory but charges were never preferred.

According to the prosecution, Philip had planned his father's murder with three accomplices, Janet Johnstoun, George Thomson and Helen Dickson, all of whom enjoyed his lavish use of his father's money. However, despite strong suspicions that they had been amongst the persons involved in the fracas witnessed by the minister, John Bell, none of them made any confessions even when subjected to torture with thumb-screws. For this reason, they were not present in the court either in the witness-box or at the bar.

None of the evidence presented could be considered sufficient to sustain a charge of murder and the prosecution case was pinned on the 'proof' provided by the ordeal by touch. However, Sir Patrick Hume, one of the counsel for the accused, urged 'that this is but a superstitious observation without any ground either in law or reason.' He related that several persons had been unjustly challenged in the past, and that he, in his own experience, had seen a dead body bleed, in presence of a person who was not guilty . . . 'And the truth is, the occasion of the dead body's bleeding was, that the chirurgion that came out to visit the body did make an incision about the neck, which might be the occasion of the bleeding;—and also the very moving of the dead body, when it was taken out of the grave and out of the coffin, might occasion the bleeding; especially, seeing the body did not bleed for some time after, which certain was made by the motion and by the incision; As also, a further evidence that it could not be the defender's touching the body, the chirurgions did lykewais touch the body, as well as he, and several others present; so that the bleeding could no more be ascribed to his touching, than the touching of the other persons present.'

The Lord Advocate, Sir James Dalrymple (later the First Earl of Stair) replied that 'as there could no natural reason be given, but an ordinar and wonderful providence of God in this kind of discovery of Murder, so the fact was never more evident and sure. Though half a dozen of persons were bearing the Corpse, no man's hands were bloody but the pannels! That the Corpse being two entire days in the grave, in that weather and

44

season, the blood, by the course of nature, was become stagnant and congealed—so that the former tossing and lifting of the Corpse, and even the incision itself, had occasioned no such effusion, but only some water or gore—but upon the first touch of the pannel, the Murderer, there appeared abundance of liquid florid blood!'

The defence did not call any witnesses on their client's behalf. In fact, they even went so far as to throw up their brief before the prosecution case had been completed. The defence they had disclosed in their pleadings that Sir James had committed suicide was clearly untenable since it would require the jury to believe that before drowning himself, he had strangled himself and broken his own neck.

At the conclusion of the addresses to the jury, the Lord Advocate asked for 'an Assize of Error against the Inquest in case they should assoilize the Pannel'; which might be interpreted as a threat that if the jury acquitted the accused, they would be fined and imprisoned for wilful error! He need not have been so concerned. A unanimous verdict of guilty was returned and the court pronounced sentence of death.

While in the condemned cell, Philip Stanfield managed to obtain a stay of execution by pretending that he wished to embrace the Catholic faith. However, he found the priests no more able to obtain clemency on his behalf and he returned to his Presbyterian faith. His sentence was duly carried out on 24th February, 1688 at the Mercat Cross in Edinburgh. As a result of a slip in the rope, he came down on his knees and it was necessary to use strangulation to dispatch him. His tongue was then cut out and burned on the scaffold as a retribution for the charge of cursing his father. His right hand was cut off and sent to be spiked on the East Port of Haddington. The mutilated body was hung up in chains at the Gallow Lee between Edinburgh and Leith, 'waving with the weather while the neck will hold.' A few days later the body was found to have been cut down and thrown into a nearby ditch. It was again hung up but it mysteriously disappeared never to be seen again.

As one writer has commented, 'It will be acknowledged that, in the circumstances related [in the records of the trial] there is not a particle of valid evidence against the young man. The surgeon's opinion as to the fact of strangulation is not entitled to much regard; but, granting its solidity, it does not prove the guilt of the accused. The horror of the young man on seeing his father's blood, might be referred to painful recollection of that profligate conduct which he knew had distressed his parent . . . especially when we reflect that Stanfield would himself be impressed with the superstitious feelings of the age, and might accept the haemorrhage as an accusation by heaven on account of the concern his conduct had had in shortening the life of his father. The whole case seems to be a lively illustration of the effect of superstitious feelings in blinding justice.'

A SHOOTING ON EASTER SUNDAY

The murder of Sir George Lockhart, 1689

It is a relatively rare occurrence for a member of the justiciary to meet with a violent death. Crimes against their person appear to be subject to the same code of honour which makes the crime of parricide so rare and which makes child murderers go in greater fear of the justice meted out by their own peers than that of the law. One of the exceptions proving this rule was the death of the Lord President of the Court of Session, Sir George Lockhart.

Lockhart came from a distinguished legal family. He was admitted to the bar in 1656 and established a name for himself as a very able barrister, soon becoming a man of power and influence. His name frequently occurs in the Books of Adjournal espousing the defence in many of the notorious cases of his time. His was the voice skilfully arguing for Mitchell against the assembled lust for revenge sought by Archbishop Sharpe and his acolytes, and also in many of the cases involving charges brought against the Covenanters. As history tells us, his rhetoric was all too frequently insufficient to save them from vengeful retribution. The talents and courage of Lockhart were also employed by the Duke of Argyle at his memorable trial in 1681. Throughout his professional life, Lockhart attracted a deep enmity from Sir George Mackenzie, who became Lord Advocate in 1677. There was no single cause for his hatred but it could mostly be put down to jealousy of his superior legal abilities and Lockhart's 'guid conceit' of himself, a quality which did not endear him to many of his contemporaries.

Lockhart was appointed President of the Court of Session in 1685 and soon afterwards, was appointed a privy-councillor and a commissioner of the exchequer. Around the same time, he bought a house sited in what is now called Old Bank Close from Sir Thomas Hope. This house had an interesting history to it. It had been built in 1569 by Robert Gourlay, not a man of substance but simply a messenger-at-arms belonging to the Abbey of Holyrood. In 1581, Regent Morton was placed under guard there for two days just before his death and by coincidence, one of Lockhart's most famous clients, Argyle, spent his last night in the house before being taken to his horrific execution. It was from this house that Lockhart would, every Sunday morning, make his way up the Lawnmarket, down West Bow to the east end of the Grassmarket, and to Greyfriars Church for divine service. One of these Sundays, he met with his death at the hand of John Chiesly.

Chiesly was from a family of wealthy burgesses who owned the fertile and valuable lands around the hamlet of Dalry. In 1688, Chiesly fell into dispute with his wife, from whom he wished to be separated. There followed an acrimonious battle regarding the financial support he should continue to provide for her and their ten children. At length, the parties each consented to the claim being settled by the arbitration of Sir George Lockhart and Lord Kennay. Unfortunately, contemporary records of the Court of Session do not contain any note of the case, but it is known that a decree was granted assigning an alimony of £93 per year out of Chiesly's estate in favour of his wife and children. Chiesly, a man of strong passion, was infuriated at the decree. His relationship with his wife and family had turned so sour that he had hoped to be able to deprive them of even the most meagre support. He resolved to take vengeance on Lockhart regardless of the cost. Six months before he actually took his revenge, Chiesly informed an advocate, Mr James Stewart, of his

Sir George Lockhart of Carnwath

intention. Stewart expressed the view that 'the very imagination of such a thing was a sin before God.' However, Chiesly fiercely replied that he alone was responsible for making his own peace with God. Lockhart was informed of Chiesly's threats, but refused to take any precautions despite the fact that Chiesly had been seen trailing him up Pall Mall in London on more than one occasion. In his subsequent statements, Chiesly confessed that on each of these occasions he had been carrying a pistol under his coat awaiting a chance to shoot his intended victim.

On Easter Sunday, 31st March, 1689, Chiesly and Lockhart were both in Edinburgh. There was much excitement in the town on account of the current siege of the castle by adherents of the new government. Chiesly arose early to thoroughly clean and charge his pistol before readying himself for the journey from Dalry to Greyfriars Church. There, he saw Lockhart in his customary pew. He sat throughout the service, eyes fixed on Lockhart and his every move, though Lockhart remained totally oblivious to Chiesly's presence. After the service Chiesly followed him and his companions, Lord Castlehill and Mr Daniel Lockhart homewards, at a none too discreet distance. But still, Lockhart had not noticed him.

At the entrance to Old Bank Close, the three men were met by Dr Hay who, besides attending Lady Lockhart for a minor ailment, had been invited to Sunday lunch. As they started to walk down the alley to Lockhart's house, Chiesly immediately drew close, raised his pistol and fired into Lockhart's back. The President staggered and fell to the ground. The ball had gone through his body and out through his right breast. Lady Lockhart, who lay in her bed, sprang up on hearing the shot. Still wearing her night-dress, she helped carry her husband into the house and placed him in a chair. A large, red blood stain on Lockhart's shirt steadily increased in size as his life ebbed away. Within minutes, he was dead.

Chiesly made no attempt to escape and was immediately seized. He boasted that he was 'not wont to do things by halves' and that he had now 'taught the President how to do justice.' Because of the enormity of his crime, the Estates of Parliament which happened to be sitting at the time ordered him to be tortured to determine whether he had any accomplices. He suffered the boot and the thumbscrews with no other names coming from his lips. Having been taken 'red-hand' immediately after committing the act, he was summarily tried before the provost of Edinburgh, as sheriff within the city. The trial was a mere formality. He was sentenced to have his right hand cut off while still alive, then hanged with the fatal weapon round his neck. His hand was then to be stuck on a spike at the West Port and his body suspended in chains at the Gallow Lee.

After the sentence had been carried out as decreed, Chiesly's body mysteriously disappeared from the gallows. It was supposed at the time that it had been taken by his friends for decent burial. Its fate was never confirmed until almost a century and a half later when workmen, removing the hearthstone of a cottage in Dalry park, found a skeleton with a pistol tied round its neck. There was no doubt that these were the remains of Chiesly.

As a final indignity to his great adversary in life, Lockhart was, in death, able to deliver the insult to Mackenzie of contriving to have his last resting place in Greyfriars Churchyard at the very spot where Mackenzie had long held designs of building his own mausoleum.

———————

A FANTASTIC TALE

The murder of Captain J. Cayley, 1716

With the introduction of comprehensive taxation schemes across the country following the Act of Union, a corps of tax officials was sent out by the government now based in London to ensure that their new-found countrymen adhered strictly to the legislation. One of these commissioners of his majesty's customs was Captain John Cayley, the son of Cornelius Cayley from York. His obnoxious profession did little to endear him to the populace, their dislike being further fuelled by his vanity. He had his residence at the old Back Stairs, great flights of stone steps built on the site of St Giles Churchyard and providing access between Old Parliament Square and the Cowgate. It is thought that this may have been the route taken by Robertson when he fled from the guard in the events leading up to the Porteus riots. From there, Cayley was known frequently to be absent overnight as he was entertained by one or other of his paramours. His dalliances appeared to leave him with little prudence or discretion.

Amongst Cayley's acquaintances was a young married woman of uncommon beauty with whom he became hopelessly infatuated. Mrs Macfarlane was the wife of John Macfarlane, Writer to the Signet in Edinburgh and the daughter of Colonel Charles Straiton who was well known as a highly trusted agent of the Jacobite party and as a particular confidante of James VIII. Cayley had made himself intimately known to Mr and Mrs Macfarlane, often being entertained at their country house and, it is said, making many valuable gifts to the lady of the house.

It is impossible to offer more than speculation as to the truth contained in the scandals which connected the name of Cayley with Mrs Macfarlane. However, regardless of the truth, it is known that Cayley viciously defamed her character, making much innuendo about her pregnancy and the identity of the father. No one could offer any plasuible excuse for his scurrilous libel. Perhaps drink had made him rash; perhaps vanity made him assume a triumph which was altogether imaginary. At any rate, his remarks reached the ears of Mrs Macfarlane. She was acquainted with Cayley's landlady, Mrs Murray, whom she happened to meet one Saturday afternoon. One can only imagine the malicious delight she took in revealing the story to its unfortunate subject.

The following Tuesday, Cayley visited the Macfarlanes' house, according to friends, anxious to apologise for his rudeness. He was shown into Mrs Macfarlane's drawing room but she kept him waiting while she changed. Accounts of what happened next show some variance. However, it seems apparent that, after some polite conversation, they went through to her bed-chamber. Here, his vanity or imagination seemed to take hold of him again and caused him to repeat the derogatory remarks concerning her honour. Mrs Macfarlane took these very calmly with no display of histrionics. With what can only be described as some measure of premeditation, she withdrew to her closet to reappear with two loaded pistols. Cayley recognised them as a pair which he himself had loaned to Mr Macfarlane only a matter of days before. Mrs Macfarlane asked Cayley to leave her house. He did not treat the command at all seriously. Despite her warning that he would regret not leaving immediately, Cayley advanced towards the young woman, trying to win her round again. She fired the first of her pistols inflicting a slight wound in Cayley's left hand. The shot carried on to embed itself in the floor. His instinct for self preservation caused him to attempt to draw his sword. The sword had hardly drawn an inch from its scabbard when Mrs Macfarlane discharged the other pistol. The bullet entered Cayley's right breast, pierced his heart and stuck in his left shoulder-blade. He dropped to the floor. So close had he been to the shot that his clothing was burnt and blackened with powder.

The enormity of her crime suddenly dawned on Mrs Macfarlane. She dropped the pistols to the floor, immediately left the room, locking the door behind her and sent one of the servants to summon her husband from the change-house where he was conducting business. On his return home, about an hour after the shooting, Mrs Macfarlane explained the circumstances which led to the bloody act. Seeing the need for prompt action, Macfarlane went out again to consult with some of his friends. They advised that he should arrange for his wife to leave the city, to prevent her being immediately placed under arrest, and to allow a precognition to be taken which would show the murder in the proper context of the events which had occasioned it. Macfarlane gathered together what money he could and around six o'clock, left the house with his wife. They walked together down the High Street to put Mrs Macfarlane on a coach. She was carried off into the night never to be seen again.

Macfarlane wandered the streets of the city, eventually returning home after ten o'clock. He issued orders that the magistrates be informed of the discovery of Cayley. Their officer was immediately dispatched to view the body and to secure the house and anybody in it who might be able to provide evidence. The magistrates themselves arrived the next day. They found Cayley lying just as he had fallen, the advanced state of rigor mortis making it difficult to straighten the body to examine the fatal wound.

A careful examination was conducted into the affair, without satisfactory explanation. Macfarlane's declarations of complete ignorance till he saw the body in his wife's bedroom which he made before the Lords of Justiciary, were accepted. Criminal letters were raised against Mrs Macfarlane by the Lord Advocate at the instigation of the father and brother of the murdered customs officer, considering there to be, at least a *prima facie* case for her to answer. Not appearing for trial, she was declared an outlaw.

What happened to Mrs Macfarlane is only open to conjecture. The only trace reported is little short of marvellous. Margaret Swinton, who was an aunt of Sir Walter Scott's mother, would rejoice in her later life, in relating a fantastic story to the young children of the family. It concerned the strange events of one Sunday morning she had been left at home by her parents when they went off to church. The young Margaret had grown tired of the loneliness of her own room and stole quietly downstairs into the parlour. There, very much to her surprise, she saw a young, beautiful woman sitting at the table drinking tea. Being an impressionable girl, she believed the woman to be one of the fairy queens so often described in her nursery tales. The apparition, after a pause of surprise, recovered her self-possession and talked quietly with the girl. She entreated her particularly to mention the meeting to nobody but her mother. Margaret turned towards the window seeking the return of her parents. She turned back again and the lady had gone. The whole event appeared like a dream.

Almost immediately her parents returned, Margaret took her mother aside and recounted her story. She was praised for obeying the request for secrecy. Her mother suggested that to do otherwise might cost the lady her life. Her mother did nothing to dispel the fantasy created in the young girl's mind. Explanations as Margaret grew older caused her to become aware that it had not in fact been a fairy queen she had seen, but the unfortunate Mrs Macfarlane. Having some blood relationship with the Swintons, she had been taken in by them and kept in a secret room till such time as she could make good a complete escape. The room in question was hidden behind the wainscot by a sliding panel— hence her ability to just disappear and so heighten Margaret's belief in the fairy story she had created for herself.

Scott used the story as part of his novel, *Peveril of the Peak*. Additionally, he considered it certain that in due course, Mrs Macfarlane was able to return to Edinburgh where she lived and died. There is no evidence to substantiate this. But, the romantic nature of the tale and the fact of the victim being an Englishman and an excise officer to boot, would certainly cause any who found it to be true to maintain his counsel.

———————

BROUGHTON'S IGNOMINY

The case of Robert Irvine, 1717

Until the latter half of the eighteenth century, the view
northwards from the Old Town of Edinburgh
encompassed thatched cottages and farm fields where
corn grew and animals grazed. Immediately beyond the
North Loch, now Princes Street Gardens, lay the grass
fields of Bearford's Parks and Woods Farm. The latter
was crossed, obliquely, by a road running over the slopes
where now is found York Place, to the village of
Broughton. This baronial burgh with its own Tolbooth
and court-house was considered to be so far afield that
people from the town would go there in the summer in
the belief that they had moved some distance away from
their normal life and surroundings.

The village has a long history. It is first mentioned in a
charter of David I, around 1143, granting the lands to
Adam Bothwell, Bishop of Orkney, who surrendered
them to Sir Lewis Bellenden, Lord Justice Clerk and
Keeper of Linlithgow Palace, in 1587.

Like other barons, the feudal superior had powers of
jurisdiction over his vassals, stretching even to the so-
called power of 'pit and gallows' which permitted the
hanging of men on a gibbet and drowning women in a pit
if their crimes so dictated. Broughton became the site of
many horrendous executions of people charged with
being witches, requiring them to be burnt alive.

It was while under the authority of the Barons of
Broughton that the village became the scene, in 1717, of a

remarkable case of murder and subsequent trial which made famous the old pathway which was located behind the later site of Register House and in which was built 'Ambrose's Tavern'. This pathway lay on the road between Silvermills, a rural hamlet on the course of the Water of Leith, and the passage into the Old Town round the dam of the North Loch. That the name of 'Gabriel's Road' should have been subsequently applied to this pathway is legendary foible, for the murderer was one Robert Irvine.

Mr James Gordon of Ellon in Aberdeenshire had a villa on the north of the city somewhere between the road to Silvermills and the village of Broughton. He was a rich merchant in Edinburgh, a one-time bailie, and the proud father of two sons and a daughter. He determined that his sons, John and Alexander, should obtain the adequate education which he could well afford, and took on as their tutor a licentiate of the church, Robert Irvine. Irvine was hard-working and a reasonably accomplished teacher but appeared to have a rather gloomy and depressive side to his nature. His mind had been taken hold of by works he had read in the college library on predestiny. He must have already entertained some degree of mental infirmity to allow such external factors to play such an important part in determining his moods and demeanour.

Also in the employ of the Gordons was a pretty, young servant-maid whose principal duties were to attend to the needs of the lady of the house. Irvine would take such opportunities as he could to see this young girl but on one occasion his pupils saw him take rather more liberty than he ought. The event was mentioned incidentally by the boys to their father, without any thought of malice, but James Gordon thought it wise to raise the matter with Irvine. On receiving a mild reprimand, Irvine apologised and Gordon, fully appreciating the attractions of the girl, forgave the indiscretion. There the matter might have ended but for the morbid and sensitive nature of Irvine. The affront to his pride, or the rebuke, sank deep and he became obsessed with a desire for revenge. He evolved the idea of going so far as to murder the boys and the chance to accomplish this was presented to him but three days later, on 28th April, 1717.

It was a pleasant Sunday afternoon. Mr and Mrs Gordon had taken their daughter to visit friends in the city. The servants had been given the afternoon free since their services would not again be required until the early evening. As usual, Irvine was left in charge of John and Alexander. He decided to take them for a walk on the nearby grassy slopes of Multrie's hill, ostensibly to combine a pleasant afternoon's walk with some nature study.

As the boys were allowed to run around gathering flowers and chasing butterflies, Irvine was considering his plan. He sat down on a rock and began whetting the knife with which he meant to destroy them. He called them over and started to castigate them for informing their father of his advances towards the maid. They stood, oblivious to Irvine's designs. Thinking he was finished, the boys ran off but he easily overtook them and seized them, throwing them to the ground. He knelt over them and, keeping one down on the grass with his knee, he cut the other's throat. He watched as the young boy bled to death. The young brother struggled to free himself but to no avail. He was hysterical with fear when Irvine brought the knife to his throat to mete out the same treatment. Within five minutes, both boys lay in pools of blood. Irvine stood unemotional, avenged.

By one of these often-encountered freak chances, a gentleman out for a stroll on the Castle Hill was surveying the northern outlook through a telescope. He obtained a perfect view of the whole episode and immediately raised the alarm. Irvine unsuccessfully tried to cut his own throat and had to flee from his pursuers.

He headed towards the Water of Leith with thoughts of drowning himself, but before he could reach it, he was captured. He was taken by cart to be imprisoned in Broughton Tolbooth where he was chained to the floor like a wild animal.

At that time, the local judiciary were allowed to hear cases of murder under summary procedure provided that the murderer 'was taken Red-hand, that is to say immediately committing the Murder, in which case he must proceed against him within three Suns.' Irvine was accordingly brought before the baron of Broughton on 30th April and received sentence of death and was immediately taken back to the tolbooth to await execution of the sentence later the same day.

In his last dying confession, supposed to be unique for a prisoner taken red-hand, it is recorded that Irvine desired one who was present to take care of his books and to conceal his papers, for, he said, there were many foolish things in them. He imagined that he was to be hung in chains and appeared to show inordinate concern on that account. He prayed that the parents of his victims

Remains of the village of Old Broughton, 1852

forgive him. At the sight of the blood-smeared clothes of the young boys brought to confront him in the prison and to further exacerbate his agonies, he broke down. The tolbooth was filled with the sound of his imprecations.

Late in the afternoon, Irvine was taken to the place of execution at Greenside. He prayed in a low voice along with the accompanying ministers. His hands were cut off by the executioner using the murder weapon and stuck on the gibbet. He was then strung up by his neck. The wound he had inflicted on his throat in his vain attempt to do away with himself opened up and blood spurted out as his heart pumped life away. After being left to hang for some days, allowing the carrion of the air to feast on his carcass, his body was flung into a neighbouring quarry hole.

———————————

THE PORTEOUS RIOTS

The lynching of Captain John Porteous, 1736

There can be few murders carried through in such public circumstances or for which a more full and colourful picture can be painted than that of Captain John Porteous. And yet, not a single person was ever successfully prosecuted for the act. Notwithstanding his own more odious personal traits, it may, with some justice, be claimed that he became just a dispensable pawn in a much greater battle between the Scots populace and the British parliament located in the remote English capital. Unfortunately for the true historian, the story has been romantically recounted by Sir Walter Scott in his novel *Heart of Midlothian*. His licence with the facts has lent the perpetrators some respectability which they, truthfully, did not merit. To provide the background, it is necessary to consider, first, events which did not directly affect Porteous.

The union of the Scots and English parliaments was met with much popular resistance which was born of pride, prejudice and a general malaise that Scotland would be destined to give up more than she had resigned in the Treaty. She would be doomed to be a slave rather than an ally of her larger sister. For many years afterwards, there occurred several incidents, irritating to the Scots, which did little to assuage their fears. Not the least of these lay in matters fiscal and the various schemes devised for exacting taxes from the Scots.

Initially, all the new commissioners of excise and custom were Englishmen who carried out their duties in rigorous fashion. Slowly, Scots started to join their ranks. However, it was maintained, these were Scotsmen chosen on account of their treachery to the true interests of Scotland and, as a result, they received little support from the local authorities. Regardless of their nationality, the officials, as well as the systems they represented and administered, incurred the odium of the whole community. A major consequence was the rise and growth of the extent of smuggling throughout the country for which its extensive coastline presented ample opportunity. The revenue officials were utterly powerless to repress, or even check, the illegal traffic since the whole community tended to thwart rather than assist their task.

The plethora of small seaports round the coast of Fife was much frequented by daring smugglers. One of the more daring of these traders in contraband was Andrew Wilson who lived at Path-head. Accompanied by George Robertson, a young stable lad from near the Bristo Port, and another Edinburgh man, William Hall, he broke into the lodgings being occupied in Pittenweem by James Stark, the collector of customs for the East Neuk. Wilson had been determined to avenge various seizures and fines he had recently suffered on account of his nefarious activities. Despite successfully escaping with two hundred pounds, the authorities had strong suspicions who the culprits were and within three days, the men were apprehended and brought to Edinburgh under strong guard.

Wilson, Robertson and Hall were tried on 2nd March 1736 and condemned to death, execution being set for 14th April. Hall subsequently had his sentence commuted to transportation for life 'solely on account of his ingenuous and candid role.' However, to the undisguised delight of the authorities, there was virtually no likelihood of such clemency being extended to his co-defendants.

To men of the daring and determination of smugglers, the opportunities for escape soon became apparent. Somehow, they managed to obtain a spring saw and with the help of two horse stealers who were imprisoned in the cell immediately above them, Wilson and Robertson succeeded in cutting through the iron bars of one of the prison windows. The other inmates of the Tolbooth assisted them by singing psalms to drown the noise of the operation. One of the horse-stealers was first to effect his escape. Wilson insisted on going next but, being a stout and bulky man, he stuck fast between the bars, unable to move forward or back. It was thus necessary to call the prison guard.

Despite his criminal tendencies, there must yet have been some noble qualities to Wilson's character, for he displayed deep and genuine grief at spoiling the young Robertson's chances of escape. He resolved to find some way of saving his comrade's life in the remaining five days before the appointed day for their execution, regardless of whatever the consequences might be for his own miserable existence. He sat in his cell silently brooding over possible plans.

Two days later, in accordance with the custom of taking condemned men to divine service on the Sabbath prior to their execution, Wilson and Robertson were escorted to the Tolbooth Church. At the end of the service, the party prepared to leave when Wilson, a man of considerable strength, managed to seize two of the soldiers guarding them with his hands and the third with his teeth. Robertson quickly managed to get away, escaping by the President's Steps to the Cowgate. He is believed to have made his way ultimately to Holland from where, ironically, he acted as a private informer for Customs House officers in Scotland.

Needless to say, the sympathies of the citizens of Edinburgh were strongly behind the prisoners, victims of the despised excise laws, and none made any attempt to

The City Guard

apprehend the fugitive. The success of the daring
achievement doubly secured Wilson's fate. However, it
excited so much admiration amongst the populace that it
became rumoured that there might be an attempt to
rescue Wilson at his execution. On Monday 12th April,
the Lord Provost ordered John Porteous, Captain of the
City Guard, to take every precaution to prevent a rescue.
He was instructed to call out the whole Guard being
further advised that powder and shot would be made
available.

Porteous was originally trained as a tailor by his father
but he was so obviously unsuited to the trade that he was
sent off to the army. After seeing service with the Scots
Brigade in Holland, he returned home to work his way
through a variety of occupations before gaining a post in
the City Guard. In due course, he gained a commission,
largely because of his accommodating the Lord Provost's
wish to be relieved of his mistress by agreeing to marry
the unfortunate woman. While still of relatively lowly
position with the Guard, he maintained an agreeable
demeanour. However, once he had advanced to a position

of honour and power, his innate characteristics came to the fore. He was a man of harsh and profligate manner, hated by the population for the severity with which he dealt with the excesses and misdemeanours of the ordinary citizens as against the extreme leniency shown to the rich and influential. It is unfortunate that the magistrates did not have a more diplomatic representative to take charge of the delicate duty of guarding Wilson's execution. Porteous is said to have taken Robertson's escape as a personal insult. Subdued fury already coursing round his veins, he was particularly incensed to find that the magistrates had arranged for a detachment of the Welsh fusiliers to be present in the principal street of the city from early in the morning of the day of execution. He resented the imputation on the ability of the City Guard and the infringement of his own dignity as their commanding officer.

Needless to say, Wilson became the butt for the surly, brutal mood which engulfed him. According to reports, as if possessed by an evil spirit, he showed diabolical, physical cruelty towards Wilson as they readied to leave the Tolbooth for the place of execution. The scene which greeted them in the Grassmarket was impressive and awe-inspiring by any standards. The whole area was packed with a vast throng filling the streets and craning from windows, strangely and ominously silent. Though the atmosphere was electric, Wilson's execution passed off without incident until it came to the moment for the cutting down of the body. Suddenly, the excitement boiled over and without warning the crowd began to throw stones and anything else which came to hand at the City Guard and started to press towards the scaffold. Porteous found personal refuge in the midst of his guard but becoming increasingly infuriated, he seized a musket and fired into the crowd, ordering his men to do the same. Porteous' shot felled one of the purported ring-leaders, Charles Husband—the man who had cut down

The Porteous Mob.

Wilson's body. The full volley killed three and wounded twelve. The crowd checked long enough for the Guard to begin to retreat up the West Bow. However, an Edinburgh mob was never easily intimidated. They pressed onwards, incensed. A second time, Porteous ordered the Guard to turn and fire. Another three people fell dead. Amongst those injured were some of the better class of citizens viewing the tumult from their windows, having taken no active part in the riot.

On return to the Guardhouse, Porteous made straight for the tavern where the magistrates were conducting business to make his report. Several thought it inexcusable that Porteous should have ordered the Guard to fire without their express authority. Public animosity and indignation were directed against Porteous from all sides. After an inquiry, the Lord Provost ordered Porteous to be detained to stand trial. Although representations were made for Porteous to stand trial under summary procedure before the Lord Provost as Sheriff, these were rejected and he appeared on indictment at the High Court of Justiciary on charges of murder, manslaughter, maiming and wounding.

To some extent, the verdict was a foregone conclusion, though there was considerable debate, bristling with dialectic subtleties, on the relevancy of the charge. Throughout the trial, the *Caledonian Mercury* conducted a constant campaign of vilification about which Porteous made special protests. However, all the rhetoric was to no avail. The jury unanimously found Porteous guilty and he was sentenced to be hanged in the Grassmarket on the afternoon of Wednesday 8th September, 1736.

Caring little for the soundness of the charges and the verdict, Edinburgh citizens were well satisfied with the fate their *bete-noire* was destined to meet. However, Porteous had cultivated some powerful friends during his sojourn in the City Guard, who regarded the proof of his guilt as doubtful. Intercessions were made on his behalf

The City Guard-House

to Queen Caroline who was acting as regent during the absence of her husband, George II, on the continent. A reprieve for six weeks, preparatory to the grant of a full pardon, was sent down from the Home Office. This action increased the indignation already felt in the capital. It was regarded as incontrovertible proof that the English government held Scottish lives in low esteem and it was promptly resolved that Porteous should not be allowed to escape the punishment he richly deserved.

Gossip and rumour, fuelled by the imprecations of the city's clergy, was so open that it eventually reached the ears of Captain Lind of the City Guard who reported the matter to the Lord Provost. He received no immediate orders. During the following few days, the Lord Provost resolutely continued to regard Lind's fears as groundless. Throughout, the intelligence deliberately let out by the principal conspirators pointed towards some occurrence on 8th April, the original date set for Porteous' execution. News of the rumours reached Porteous, but like the Lord Provost, he steadfastly refused to believe any of it.

Between nine and ten o'clock in the evening of Tuesday 7th April, just before the closing of the ports, a band of men gathered in the Portsburgh and, forcing the city drummer to lead their procession, they marched into the city by the West Port, the gates of which were nailed and barricaded shut behind them. They marched along the Cowgate to the Cowgate Port, their numbers increasing at every step as if following a pre-arranged plan. The Cowgate Port was secured and men were despatched to similarly secure the Bristo and Potterrow Ports while the main body of the accumulating crowd headed for the Netherbow Port to cut off all communications with, and the access of, the Welsh Fusiliers quartered in the Canongate. A strong party was left to hold this important post and the rest of the mob rushed back up the High Street to the Tolbooth, ransacking the City Guardhouse on the way of all its weapons. A party was assigned the task of silencing the bell of St Giles lest the magistrates had a mind to ring it to summon assistance.

The city magistrates tried to read the riot act but were frightened off by the guards placed across the High Street both east and west of the Tolbooth to prevent interruption during the assault on its outer door. The crowd were in no mood to listen to any pleas for reason. They had long since been carried away with the fervour and atmosphere of the occasion. In any case, considering the strength of feeling against Porteous pervading the city, it is unlikely that it would have taken much to dissuade any intervention. The magistrates found no one prepared to undertake the perilous task of carrying written orders summoning help either from the garrisons stationed in the castle or the forces under Colonel Moyle in the Canongate. The only effort made in this direction was a verbal approach by the M.P. for the city, Mr Patrick Lindsay, who had managed to scale a section of the city walls to reach the Canongate. Moyle allowed his own discretion to prevail and refused Lindsay's requests to intervene. Besides, he would have been disinclined to make any move without the written authority of the Lord Chief Justice whose residence was some five miles distant.

For nearly an hour, the door of the Tolbooth resisted all attempts with sledge-hammer and crowbar to breach it. The crowd grew impatient. Tar-barrels and other combustible materials were summoned. The door finally succumbed. By 11.30 p.m., the Tolbooth was in the hands of the crowd. The jailer's keys were procured and though they could hardly see each other for smoke, the ring-leaders found Porteous' cell, having unlocked all other cells on the way, releasing the other detainees in the jail.

Although Walter Scott would have us believe that the rioters treated Porteous with the consideration he had denied Wilson and at all times let him keep his composure, such is far from the truth. The mercies of a rampaging mob bent on revenge are barbarities and cruelties. Porteous was dragged by the legs down the stairs to the street below, his head banging down each step. Then, pushed from behind and pulled by the arms, he was taken up the Lawnmarket to the Bowhead. The crowd stopped for a little, some wishing to have the deed done then and there. This was rejected by their leaders who pressed on down the West Bow. All around, the crowd, thirsty to reek their vengeance, shouted and chanted. Their acquired muskets were fired into the air. Burning torches were run round Porteous' face and the mob beat and punched him mercilessly. The procession halted at the shop of a dealer in cordage, broke in and selected a coil of rope. They surged on to the Grassmarket, the usual place of execution. It was found crowded with rioters, crimson with the light from a mass of flickering torches, spectators filling every window of the tall houses, the castle standing high above the tumult amidst the blue midnight and the stars.

Only the massive sandstone block with its square hole for the gallows stood in the appointed place. Despite impressions that hanging was a penalty frequently meted out to offenders, it was not so prevalent that the gallows were permanently erected. In the search for a suitable gibbet, a dyer's pole was found in the immediate vicinity and was pressed into service as the instrument for what was considered to be the lawful murder of Porteous. The rope was thrown over the pole. Porteus begged for mercy and entreated the mob to permit him to pray. His requests were denied, the mob declaring that he had never prayed for himself in the past and that he should be damned before he got the time to do so now. The rope was tied round his neck and he was immediately hauled up. He hung for three minutes then was let down again, still alive. His nightgown and shirt were ripped off and tied round his head. To loud cheering, he was pulled up again. His hands and arms had not been tied so he was able to struggle and writhe about on the end of his rope. One of the crowd put a stop to that by smashing his right arm and shoulder with the Lochaber axe he had taken from the Guardhouse. The crowd continued to pull Porteous up and down for the best part of an hour. Each time he received more brutal treatment, a punch, a kick, a stab in the side, burning with a torch. When it was obvious that his life was extinguished, the end of the rope was wound round one arm of the makeshift gallows and nailed in place, Porteous' body was left swinging in the breeze. The spectacle over, the rioters dispersed into the night as quickly as the original band had gathered in Portsburgh.

When morning dawned over the city, the gaping hole that was once the gateway to the Tolbooth, a litter of discarded weapons about the streets and the silent figure swaying at the pole were the only traces of the ugly and fantastic dream.

The government demanded a full enquiry. However, the magistrates, relieved to see order restored and still stunned by the collective feelings of the mob, had little heart for it and paid but lip service to the demand. They also realised the futility of trying to conduct such an enquiry, for there is no doubt that no one would have been prepared to provide any evidence of complicity against any person charged. The Lord Advocate, Duncan Forbes, was obliged to come to Edinburgh from his residence at Culloden. The Queen offered a pardon to any turning King's evidence and a reward of £200 was offered for information leading to the apprehension and conviction of any implicated in the murder of Porteous. There were no takers. The law officers of the Crown redoubled their efforts to trace any clue which might lead them to discovering the identity of any of the ringleaders. They met with complete failure. Not one was ever detected.

Only two men were ever brought to trial for alleged involvement. William McLauchlan, a footman to the Countess of Wemyss and a man of low mental capacity, was able to prove that he had been drunk (and virtually unconsciously so) when caught in the wash of the passing rabble and compelled to accompany them. Charges against Thomas Linnen were not brought to trial until two years after the event. Like McLaughlan, he was also acquitted.

The only party to suffer any penalty was the city itself. Initially, to try to preserve the city's good name and in order to salve their own consciences, the magistrates granted a pension to the destitute widow. The government was unimpressed and a bill was brought before parliament aimed at imposing serious sanctions against Edinburgh. Fortunately, during the extensive debate, the more iniquitous provisions were dropped and a fine of £2000 was levied for the benefit of Porteous' widow.

To this day, the riot is still shrouded in mystery. Though the manner of the murder of Porteous is well known, the identity of the players and the details of the preparations of their plans are still maintained as secrets carried to the grave.

THE BANK MESSENGER

Death of William Begbie, 1806

Tweeddale House which has given its name to
Tweeddale Court in the city's High Street carries a long
history. It was originally built and occupied in the early
years of the seventeenth century by the same Lady Yester
whose name is attached to the church in the Canongate.
On her death, the house was bestowed on her grandson,
John, second Earl of Tweeddale (and ninth Lord Yester).
He, and his subsequent heirs to his titles and estates, used
the house as their town residence. The last of the family
to use the house was the fourth Marquis who was
Secretary of State for Scotland from 1742 to 1745. After
his death in 1762, Tweeddale House passed into the
hands of the British Linen Banking House.

The British Linen Company was originally
incorporated by a charter under the Privy Seal in 1746
when the Scots people were still reeling from the after-
effects of the '45 Rebellion and the defeat at the battle of
Culloden. A number of men of influence considered it
important to attempt to introduce some stability to the
country and its economy and chose the manufacture of
linen as being an industry likely to provide ample
employment and good financial return seeking to satisfy
the extensive home and foreign markets. The company
was established with the very broad objects allowing it to
engage in the full range of activities directly necessary
and peripheral, to the conversion of flax to linen. The
hopes for linen were not fulfilled and the company turned

74

to concentrate on the financial business which had been established for its own purposes, intent on making its services available to a wider community.

In 1806, during the British Linen's ownership of Tweeddale House took place the extraordinary and still judicially unsolved mystery of the murder of one of their porters, William Begbie. Around five o'clock on the evening of 13th November, he was found lying in the short dark passage leading into Tweeddale Court by a

Tweeddale House

young girl who had been sent to the neighbouring well for water. When the girl stumbled over the dark bundle which proved to be Begbie's body, he was still alive but on the point of expiry. The porter had been stabbed with a knife which was stuck up to the haft in his heart. The nature of the murder showed the most appalling deliberation on the part of its perpetrator. The weapon had a broad, thin blade whose rounded front had been ground to a point specifically for its foul purpose. The wooden handle of the knife had been wrapped around with soft paper so as to prevent blood from spurting from the wound when pushed fully home and thus prevent the murderer from being stained with any of his victim's blood which might provide evidence of guilt. Begbie had slowly bled to death, unable to utter a word to any single soul which could help explain the tragedy. He left a wife and four young children to mourn his cruel death. The Bank made financial provision for them and it is interesting to note that one of the boys subsequently followed his father's footsteps into the company's employ.

The motive for Begbie's murder appeared to be robbery for it was found that £4392 in bank notes which he had been carrying from the company's branch in Leith to their head office was missing. The circumstances of his death caused much excitement in the population and extensive efforts were made to identify and apprehend his murderer. No house of doubtful character remained unvisited and men patrolled all the roads out of the city. The Bank put up a reward of £500 for information which might lead to a conviction while the government promised a King's pardon to any of the murderer's accessories. The efforts met with a singular lack of success. All that could be ascertained was that while Begbie had been proceeding up Leith Walk, he seemed to have been accompanied by an unidentified man and that around the presumed time of the murder, a 'man' was seen by some children to run from the close and down Leith Wynd. There was no way of confirming that these two men were one and the same. There was also evidence that the knife had been bought around two o'clock on the afternoon of the murder and afterwards ground and sharpened on a grinding stone. The shopkeeper was unable to provide any information which might cast light on his customer's identity.

All else failing, the authorities arrested, on suspicion, a number of characters whom they considered most likely to be involved in a crime of this nature. All, with one exception, were able to give sustainable evidence of their innocence. The exception was a particularly desperate and dangerous character who plied trade as a carrier between Perth and Edinburgh. In the event, it was shown that although he had been seen in the Canongate soon after the murder, he was not implicated in Begbie's murder. He had, in fact, been engaged in other criminal activity which might have rendered him liable to capital punishment. Small wonder that he chose to remain silent.

The months rolled past. No fresh evidence was uncovered and the murder of Begbie occupied less and less of the public's attention. Out of the blue on 10th August of the following year, a mason and two friends passing through the grounds of Bellevue (a mansion situated roughly where Drummond Place now stands) found a roll of banknotes in a hole in the old surrounding wall. They immediately delivered the roll to the Sheriff Clerk's office where it was found to contain about £3000 in remarkably well preserved notes. They were identified as the same large denomination notes as those taken from William Begbie. The three men received a reward of £200 from the British Linen Company, but still no further light was shed on the actual crime. It was considered more than a little curious that one of the finders actually lived where the murder had been committed, but he was able to prove he had not been in Edinburgh at the relevant time.

Although strictly speaking the murder remains unsolved to this day, there is a strange sequel to the story which came closest to providing the identity of the murderer, though irrefutable proof still remained out of reach. In June 1820, at the High Court of Justiciary, a certain James Mackoull was sentenced to death for robbing a branch of the Paisley Union Bank in Glasgow of £20,000. Despite reprieve, Mackoull died in Calton jail around the turn of the year. Some eighteen months later, the superintendent of the Leith police, a Bow Street runner by the name of Denovan, published a paper which purported to prove that Mackoull was the murderer of Begbie. His thesis was based on a statement from a man he had discovered working in Leith as a teacher but who, in 1806, had been a sailor boy and who, it was claimed, had witnessed events bearing directly on the case. His statement was as follows:

'I was at that time a boy of fourteen years of age. The vessel to which I belonged had made a voyage to Lisbon and was then lying in Leith harbour. I had brought a small present from Portugal for my mother and my sister, who resided in the Netherbow, Edinburgh, immediately opposite to Tweeddale's Close, leading to the British Linen Company's Bank. I left the vessel late in the afternoon, and as the articles I had brought were contraband, I put them under my jacket, and was proceeding up Leith Walk, when I perceived a tall man carrying a yellow-covered parcel under his arm, and a genteel man, dressed in a black coat, dogging him. I was a little afraid: I conceived the man who carried the parcel to be a smuggler, and the gentleman who followed him to be a custom-house or excise officer. In dogging the man, the supposed officer went from one side of the Walk to the other, as if afraid of being noticed, but still kept about the same distance behind him. I was afraid of losing what I carried, and shortened sail a little, keeping my eyes fixed on the person I supposed to be an officer, until I came to the head of Leith Street, when I saw the smuggler take the North Bridge, and the custom house officer go in front of the Register Office; here he looked round him, and imagining he was looking for me, I hove to, and watched him. He then went the same way. I stood a minute or two where I was, and then went forward, walking slowly up the North Bridge. I did not, however, see either of the men before me; and when I came to the south end, or head of the Bridge, supposing that they might have gone up the High Street or along the South Bridge, I turned to the left, and reached the Netherbow, without again seeing either the smuggler or the officer. Just, however, as I came opposite to Tweeddale's Close, I saw the custom-house officer come running out of it with something under his coat: I think he ran down the street. Being much alarmed, and supposing that the officer had also seen me and knew what I carried, I deposited my little present in my mother's with all possible speed, and made the best of my way to Leith, without hearing anything of the murder of Begbie until next day. On coming on board the vessel, I told the mate what a narrow escape I conceived I had made: he seemed somewhat alarmed (having probably, like myself, smuggled some trifling article from Portugal), and told me in a peremptory tone that I should not go ashore alone again without first acquainting him. I certainly heard of the murder before I left Leith, and concluded that the man I saw was the murderer; but the idea of waiting on a magistrate and communicating what I had seen never struck me. We sailed in a few days thereafter from Leith; and the vessel to which I belonged having been captured by a privateer, I was carried to a French prison, and only regained my liberty at the last peace. I can now recollect distinctly the figure of the man I saw; he was well dressed, had a genteel appearance, and wore a black coat. I never saw his face properly, for he was before me the whole way up the Walk; I think, however, he was a stout, big man, but not so tall as the man I then conceived to be a smuggler.'

Although not uniquely distinctive, Denovan adduced that the description provided by his witness exactly matched that of Mackoull. However, further coincidences are related which add weight to his theory. Mackoull was a rogue hailing originally from London who for some time had frequented various parts of Scotland carrying out the most daring robberies. He was known to have stayed in Edinburgh from 1805 through to the end of 1806, having been frequently seen in the Ship Tavern in Leith. Although he claimed to be a merchant from Hamburg with particular interests in the leather trade, he was in reality more acquainted with the crafts of gambler and pickpocket. While in Edinburgh, he rented very modest lodgings at the foot of New Street, to which, perhaps circumstantially, the quickest and quietest access from Tweeddale's Close would have been by Leith Wynd. Strangely, Mackoull was not included in the number detained for questioning at the time of the murder.

For Denovan, the clinching evidence supporting Mackoull's guilt came from a conversation he had with him in the condemned cell prior to the prisoner's reprieve. According to his report of the meeting: 'He [Denovan] told Captain Sibbald [the superior of the prison] that he intended to ask Mackoull a single question relative to the murder of Begbie, but would first humour him by a few jokes, so as to throw him off his guard, and prevent him from thinking he had called for any particular purpose; but desired Captain Sibbald to watch the features of the prisoner when he [Denovan] put his hand to his chin, for he would then put the question he meant.' After talking for some time, Denovan posed the very simple question: 'By the way, Mackoull, if I am correct, you resided at the foot of New Street, Canongate, in November 1806, did you not?' Mackoull was at first stunned. He then threw himself back on the bed as if in a convulsion. Amid a torrent of expletives, he strongly denied even being in Edinburgh at the time, though proceeded to contradict himself as to where he actually was. He continued to rave in his agitated state and Denovan left the cell.

Although largely circumstantial, the evidence seems to point to the fact of Mackoull being the murderer of William Begbie. However, one question which appears not to have been addressed is that, given the obvious premeditation to the act, how did the murderer know that at that time, on that day, a porter of the British Linen Bank would be carrying such a large sum of money, unescorted, to Tweeddale Court?

AT A HOUSE OF ILL REPUTE

The stabbing of William Howatt, 1828

All too often throughout the early periods of the development of Scottish legal history and practice, court records are sadly lacking or indeed completely missing for many cases whose details would have been of interest not only to the obscure legal researcher, but also to historians hoping to paint pictures of life in the different strata of Scottish society. However, against that can be set the considerably different approach of the media of the day. Whereas today, we are very much conditioned to obtaining much of our information about contemporary events from visual images, the written word used to be the only way of communicating. This meant, for example, a very high standard of detailed reporting of events. Thus, certainly as far as court cases were concerned, a very much more interesting and wider-ranging description can be obtained from a contemporary newspaper report than any purely factual court record could ever present. It was also common to produce broadsheets or pamphlets consonant on any event which had attracted, or was sure to attract, the lurid attentions of the public. One such event was the trial of Mary Mackinnon for the alleged murder of William Howatt which, to no small degree, owed its popular interest to the character and profession of the principal. The case also had an extremely interesting aftermath which even with today's comprehensive court reporting could easily be missed as part of the complete story.

Mystery surrounds Mary's origins. She was generally believed to have been born in Ireland, about thirty-two years before the events which were to impress her name on history, the daughter of a soldier. She visited St Helena, South Africa and the East Indies as the family followed her father's successive postings. When only fifteen, her mother died and her fall from the straight and narrow began at her mother's funeral when, as her father lay helplessly drunk, Mary was seduced by a young officer who had been showing inordinate interest in her for some time. Not much more than a year later, her father left the army and the family settled in Glasgow. There, she fell in with a series of acquaintances who cared as much for her reputation as the young officer at her mother's funeral. She enjoyed the attention and the havoc she could create in the emotions of the young men playing court to her. Unsurprisingly, she stretched the forebearance of her father to such an extent that she opted to leave home rather than to knuckle down to the somewhat belated attempts to exert authority over her behaviour.

The next substantiated report of Mary's life is that of her return to Scotland in 1812 after moving round with the armies in Europe. Under the name of Mrs Mackinnon, she opened a 'house of ill repute' at 82 South Bridge. She carried on business, seeking to attract a more up-market clientele, with a reasonable degree of success for approaching eleven years.

In February 1823, Henry Ker and William Howatt held a dinner party at the house they occupied in Broughton Street for a number of their business acquaintances. During the course of the evening, several bottles of whisky were consumed and all were distinctly drunk when it came time for one of the number, James Johnston, to make his way home to Bristo. Although each of the guests was to subsequently deny the extent of his own intoxication, there was general agreement that William Howatt was certainly not the least affected. The revellers decided that they would accompany Johnston on his walk up the Bridges with the intention of playing a joke on him. They all knew of Johnston's sheltered up-bringing and his rather prudish attitudes, and thought to engineer his entry into Mrs Mackinnon's house. Opposite to it, there stood premises occupied by a boxer's club and it was there, it was suggested, that they ought to repair for a final drink before reaching Johnston's home. However, he appeared to have an abhorrence of physical violence, whatever its guise, and he refused to accompany them. He insisted on going to a more respectable place. It is hard to believe that he was so ingenuous that he had not heard of Mrs Mackinnon's or realised the true nature of her particular drinking house. However, he more readily agreed to join his companions in a drink there.

It did not take him too long to realise the trick that had been played upon him as the serving girls individually served drinks to each of them and displayed considerably more attention to the alehouse's customers than he had ever previously encountered. He was not at all pleased at the ruse played upon him and left in anger, knocking over unoccupied tables in his haste. His companions remained enjoying their trick at Johnston's expense and ordered more drink. It was during the next half an hour that the incident was to occur which was to put an end to Mary Mackinnon's sordid business interests.

At the subsequent trial, prosecution witnesses' evidence showed slight variations in their views, or recollections, of events. According to some of the girls in Mrs Mackinnon's 'licensed tavern', their Madam was out visiting friends when William Howatt and his friends arrived already well oiled, though still able to walk without assistance. The men ordered a jug of toddy which they shared with some of the girls. When it was finished, another was ordered. In the meantime, Johnston had completed his escape and the girls had locked the front door to prevent any other members of the party leaving. Most repaired to the kitchen to attend to the preparation of the new jug of toddy and it was here that what had been relatively good-humoured repartee turned nasty when one of the girls, Elizabeth McDonald, who was known to have a quick temper, turned on Henry Ker, objecting to the manner of approaches he was making to her. She tore at his shirt and knocked him down behind the kitchen door. No sooner had he picked himself up, than he was set upon again. His companions came to his aid while, not unnaturally, some of the other girls sought to help their own friend. Some claimed that candlesticks were picked up as weapons, either defensive or offensive. Fighting continued in the kitchen and the passageway as Mrs Mackinnon returned. She immediately gave full vent to her anger, having already heard the noise of the fracas from the street. She forced her way through the bodies in the passageway to the kitchen and deliberately selected a knife from a drawer in the kitchen dresser. The next fatal step carried conflicting reports, varying from self defence to a vicious attack. Either way, William Howatt now lay on the kitchen floor, blood flowing from a large wound in his chest. He was lifted to a chair and the police were called.

The police arrived in company with a doctor who was immediately shown to the kitchen where he found Howatt sitting in a state of stupor. He gave first aid to help stem the flow of blood and had him immediately conveyed to the Royal Infirmary. The police busied themselves taking note of the confused versions of the tragedy. Their task was not made easy by the drunken state of the men and the basically untrustworthy accounts of the girls, anxious not to incriminate themselves by admitting to the true reasons for their presence on the premises.

William Howatt's wounds proved too serious for him to have much hope of responding favourably to treatment. However, Sheriff Tait was able to take a dying declaration from him in which he identified Mary

Mackinnon as his assailant. His body was subjected to a routine post mortem. The pathologists noted a gash in the left ventricle of the heart and, satisfied with the cause of death, they were about to sew up their incision when one of their medical colleagues, who was present merely as an interested spectator, suggested that it might be of value to deduce the angle at which the knife had entered the chest. Careful examination determined that the knife had severed the cartilage of the second rib and penetrated to the heart, moving to the left and downwards. This small point, perhaps discovered very much by accident, was very relevant at the trial. In her preliminary statements, Mary Mackinnon claimed she had held the knife in front of her, the point sloping forwards and upwards, in an attitude of self defence, and that Howatt had stumbled towards her and on to the knife. The nature of the wound was much more consistent with the testimony of one of his companions who swore he saw the woman holding the knife like a dagger and striking down, from above her head, into the body of the unfortunate Howatt.

The evidence presented by the prosecution seemed overwhelmingly to point towards Mary Mackinnon being guilty of bringing about William Howatt's death. The great talents of her counsel, Jeffrey and Cockburn, later to become eminent judges, had to fight hard for such a hopeless case. They adopted the approach of putting some of the blame down to the behaviour of Howatt and his companions in compounding the circumstances where it was inevitable that somebody would be hurt. They argued that her action was very much one taken in the heat of the moment by a woman anxious for her own safety, that of her friends and of her house. She could not be accused of malice aforethought. The trial proceedings had lasted for fourteen hours when Jeffrey began his speech for the defence. In his journal published fifty years later Cockburn still remained moved by his

Francis, Lord Jeffrey

eloquence directed at the hearts of the jury rather than their heads. 'Mr Jeffrey concluded with a strong and energetic appeal to the feelings of the jury on behalf of the unfortunate creature, who early in life had reputation, and had been deserted by those whose reclaiming discipline might have drawn her from the dreadful course of iniquity in which she had indulged.'

However, the Lord Justice-Clerk was more matter of fact. He quite clearly guided the jury to attach more credence to the evidence of the dead man's companions as to the circumstances of his death and that, regardless of provocation, there was nothing justifiable in the prisoner's action. The jury agreed, but recommended that the court should exercise mercy. Their plea was unheeded, for she was sentenced to be executed and her body thereafter to be delivered to Dr Alexander Monro for dissection.

The execution took place on 16th april, 1823 at the head of Libberton's Wynd in the Lawnmarket, attracting a crowd estimated at twenty thousand. Cockburn recalled a strange tale surrounding Mary Mackinnon's final moments on this earth. According to his recollections, 'she died publicly, but gracefully and bravely; and her last moment was marked by a proceeding so singular, that it is on its account that I mention her case. She had an early attachment to an English Jew, who looked like a gentleman, on the outside at least; and this passion had never been extinguished. She asked him to come and see her before her fatal day. He did so; and on parting, finally, on her last evening, she cut an orange into two and, giving him one half, and keeping the other herself, directed him to go to some window opposite the scaffold, at which she could see him, and to apply his half to his lips when she applied her half to hers. All this was done; she saw her only earthly friend, and making the sign, died, cheered by his affection.'

Jeffrey and Cockburn also had another cause to remember their client. In her will, Mary Mackinnon had left everything she had, a small fortune for those days of four or five thousand pounds, to a friend, Robert Baird, an accountant in Edinburgh. He took the legacy, but refused to pay the expenses of the defence. James Rutherford, Mary's solicitor, who had instructed Jeffrey and Cockburn, brought an action against him. It was one of these issues upon which the obscurity of language and its inherent inexactness causes law and lawyers to thrive. The submission to Lord Meadowbank in the Court of Session was: 'It being admitted that the pursuer [Rutherford] was employed as agent to conduct the defence of the late Mrs Mackinnon, and did conduct her defence accordingly—whether the pursuer was so employed by, and on the credit and responsibility of the said Mrs Mackinnon? or by, and on the credit and responsibility of, the defender [Baird]? or by, and on the

credit and responsibility of, the defender and Mrs
Mackinnon jointly?' Baird argued that he did not employ
Rutherford, nor did he subsequently render himself
responsible for payment of the account, so that there was
no liability on him for Mary's defence costs. However,
Rutherford's counsel pointed out that, though frequent
demands had been made, Baird had not denied liability
until some six months after Mary's execution. In his
address to the jury, Lord Meadowbank found it difficult
to give advice, because whatever their finding, it would
have to be returned to the 'Court to find the law. If a
general issue had been sent, then a verdict upon it would
have been a warrant for judgement here. The issue would
have been, whether the defender alone, or along with Mrs
Mackinnon, understood to pay, and the jury could then
have distinctly found one way or other; but here the
question is so put, that if the jury make a return in terms
of the issue, it would be putting a point of law on the face
of the verdict. This you must try to avoid, and will find
for the pursuer or defender, according to the opinion you

have formed on the facts and circumstances.' No wonder Charles Dickens' character, Mr Micawber, felt justified in declaring, 'the law is an ass'!

The jury took the safest course of finding 'for the defender'. Who knows if Mr Rutherford ever did receive his payment?

THE WEST PORT MURDERS

The story of Burke and Hare, 1828

The realisation in the late 18th and early 19th centuries that much of the knowledge of human anatomy was empirical rather than based on scientific fact gave rise to a need for human cadavers for dissection and study. In Scotland, these were not easily available, for much superstition existed to cause the dead often to be held in greater reverence than the living. After all, at the last trump, how were the dead going to rise up if they lay dissected and pickled? The demand for bodies gave rise to a new criminal willing to obtain them for a price, the resurrectionists. The horror of relatives and the community to find a fresh grave reopened and the recently interred body of a loved one removed overnight was total.

Those caught in the act suffered the ultimate retribution. It eventually occurred to at least some of the resurrectionists that they were causing themselves unnecessary physical effort and laying themselves open to considerably increased risk of being caught by actually opening up a grave. It would be far more sensible a proposition to get the body before its committal. People could always be found who would sell a recently deceased relative rather than incur the burden of funeral expenses. However, this option carried the considerable disadvantage that if one conducted a healthy trade, there could grow up a considerable number of 'clients' who might, if suitably persuaded, testify to the existence of, and one's involvement in, such a trade. The obvious answer was to obtain the bodies by actually bringing about their owners' demise by one's own hand. So, the considerable itinerant or homeless population of the time frequently had one of their number meet an untimely death. Such a death or disappearance did not attract undue attention.

Amongst the most well known exponents of the art were William Burke and William Hare who have earned themselves immortality in the annals of Edinburgh infamy. It is perhaps not totally unexpected that such a tale could be told of Edinburgh given the reputation, established and growing throughout the world, of its medical school.

Both Burke and Hare hailed from Ireland. They came across the Irish Sea in search of work which they both found in the construction of the Union Canal, though there is no evidence to suggest that the men ever actually met each other there. It was while engaged on this work, however, that Burke did meet Helen McDougal with whom he took up living. By all accounts, the relationship

Burke and Hare

was at times stormy due, in no small measure, to the liking each had for drink. However, they had a deep affection for each other which transcended their difficult times. Hare met his wife, Mary Laird, while she was married to the proprietor of the lodging house in which he found accommodation in Edinburgh. After his landlord's death, Hare moved in with, and finally got married to, the widow, becoming the new proprietor of the house in Tanner's Close which was to achieve such notoriety. It was in these lodgings that Burke and McDougal were invited to stay when they returned to Edinburgh in the autumn of 1827 after working in the harvest round the Penicuik area.

The entry of Burke and Hare into the anatomists' supply trade was rather accidental. Amongst the residents in Tanner's Close was a pensioner by the name of Donald. He died in late 1827, owing Hare £4 to be paid from his quarterly pension which was almost due. After all the funeral arrangements had been made, it occurred to Hare that he may have difficulty in reclaiming the debt from the relatives to whom the pension would go but that by selling the body he could at least ensure his claim. When the scheme was first suggested to Burke, he was reluctant to become involved but a promise of a share of the proceeds was adequately persuasive. The men opened the coffin, removed the body and replaced it with tanner's bark. Donald was put back into his old bed. In the evening, they visited Surgeon's Square and made arrangements to deliver the body. Being new to the business, the anatomist's assistant was a little circumspect in negotiation with them. Nevertheless, the body was duly delivered later the same evening and the two men were paid £7.10s. by Dr Robert Knox who informed them that he would be glad to deal with them again in the future if the opportunity ever presented itself. The possibilities for substantially augmenting their meagre, legitimate income became all to clear to the men and their wives. The first person to fall prey to their new designs was Abigail Simpson, an old woman from Gilmerton, who had come into town to collect her weekly pension of 1s.6d. Some of her pension had already gone on drink when Hare met her and immediately formed the impression that such an old, weakly woman would be an eminently suitable subject as their first victim. He engaged her in conversation and before long, she was readily persuaded to return to his house for a drink where she was introduced to Hare's three partners. Before too long, Abigail Simpson became so drunk that she could hardly stand, let alone make her way home. It was agreed she could stay the night in Tanner's Close. Whether through their state of inebriation or lack of sufficient courage, Burke and Hare could not bring themselves to carry through their evil intentions.

The next morning, Abigail awoke with a severe hangover. She received the utmost sympathy and was offered 'a hair of the dog.' With much of last night's drink still in her, she quickly returned to helpless intoxication. The house was quiet. Courage did not now desert the men. Burke lay across the woman's body to prevent her offering any resistance. Hare placed his hand across her mouth and nose to stop her breathing. Within a few minutes, their victim was dead. They stripped the body and placed it in a chest. Later that day, it was delivered to Dr Knox who approved of its being so fresh but he asked no questions of its origin when handing over £10 in payment. Any influence that conscience might have had to play was largely dissipated now that they realised how easy and lucrative was their new profession. Other victims soon fell foul of them.

One murder which showed remarkable and brazen audacity given that it occurred so early in their career was that of Mary Paterson, a young woman well known on the streets of Edinburgh. On the morning of 9th April, 1828, Burke left the house to make for a tavern in the

Canongate. As he drank to try to get away from the depressive feeling of guilt which came over him on occasion, Mary Paterson and her friend, Janet Brown, joined him having not long been released from the local police station where they had been apprehended for being drunk and disorderly the previous night. He offered to buy them a drink which quickly became three, then invited them back to his lodgings for breakfast. Taking two bottles of whisky, they made for the house of Burke's brother in Gibb's Close. Before too long, despite a large breakfast, Burke and Paterson were quite drunk. Janet Brown, while not abstemious, was more temperate and remained in full control of herself. Mary Paterson drank herself to unconsciousness. In order to clear his head, Burke decided he should take a walk and offered to take Janet Brown with him. On their return, they found that Helen McDougal had arrived. She flew at Janet Brown for trying to practise her wiles on her husband but turned her fury on her husband when she found that it was he who had befriended the two girls. Burke managed to put his wife out of the house and then to conduct Janet

Mary Laird (Mrs Hare)   *Helen McDougall*

Brown to safety. He returned to Gibb's Close and awaited the arrival of Hare and his wife who had been summoned by Burke's sister in-law, fearful for her own life and possessions during the argument between Burke and McDougal. She did not accompany them back to her house, where Burke and Hare exercised their fatal skills on the frail and still unconscious body of Mary Paterson.

Within four hours of her death, Mary lay in Dr Knox's dissecting room with Burke and Hare £8 richer. If suspicions were aroused in the anatomist's assistants about the girl's identity or the evidence of extremely recent death, they were not brought to the attention of the authorities. For some months afterwards, Janet Brown tried to trace Mary Paterson but no one seemed to have heard anything from her since her supposed departure to Glasgow in the company of a packman. If more determined investigations had been made, Burke and Hare's grisly deeds could have been terminated forthwith, there being too many clues and witnesses available for them to sustain any fallacious defence. As it was, the matter rested for eight months until the great conspiracy against human life was brought to light.

Amongst those to fall victim in those succeeding months was James Wilson, known popularly as 'Daft Jamie', a well known figure in the area of the Grassmarket. He was 'a quiet, harmless being, and gave no person the smallest offence whatever; he was such a simpleton that he would not fight to defend himself, though he werever so ill-used, even by the smallest boy.' The murder of such a well known character can only be described as an act of the utmost folly which courted discovery. So long as they confined their activity to tramps and strangers to the city, they were comparatively safe, but now they were treading on dangerous ground.

It was Mrs Hare who came across Daft Jamie wandering round the Grassmarket searching for his mother, one morning in late September. She claimed to have seen her and invited Jamie back to her house to wait for her. Jamie followed her in all innocence. Hare offered him a drink while he waited and Mrs Hare set off, supposedly to fetch Mrs Wilson. In fact, it was Burke she was away to find. Despite his fear of ever becoming drunk, the two men managed to ply Jamie with enough whisky for him to reach a half-dazed state which caused him to feel the need to lie down. The two of them watched their intended victim to determine the safest moment to act. They knew that this case would not be as easy as previous ones. This time, they were dealing with someone young and physically strong who had, in addition, not consumed the same amount of liquor to deaden his senses and reactions. They felt the time had come to move. However, no sooner had Jamie been touched than he awoke to defend himself. There was a furious struggle between Jamie and Burke which Hare stood and watched. It was only when Burke threatened to use a knife that Hare joined the fray. Together, they managed to overcome him. Despite attempts to struggle free, Burke had him securely pinned to the ground while Hare covered his mouth. Gradually, Jamie's strength waned and his life slipped away. Burke and Hare were not without pain and bruising from the fight. They needed to rest awhile before proceeding to strip their victim and to put the body in the chest. On this occasion, they made the fatal error of keeping some of their victim's clothing and personal effects. In all the other murders, these had been destroyed to prevent detection.

In the afternoon, Jamie was taken to Surgeon's Square. Burke and Hare received £10. There is no doubt that some of the staff or students would have recognised Jamie. None of them made any public statement or questioned how Burke and Hare had come by the body. A rumour did grow amongst the public that Jamie had been seen on one of Dr Knox's dissecting tables. However, when Mrs Wilson and her friends went there, there was no trace of him.

It is not absolutely certain how many bodies were delivered by the infamous pair to Dr Knox. Various reports put it down as being between sixteen and thirty. Burke in a confession published in the *Edinburgh Evening Courant* listed sixteen for which he could provide some detail but there were undoubtedly more. The last was Mary Campbell, or Docherty, an old Irishwoman who had come to Edinburgh to look for her son. Burke, by now always on the lookout for new business, met Mrs Campbell in a shop where she was asking for information. Her obvious Irish origin gave him the perfect excuse to begin talking with her. As a ruse, he claimed that his mother's name had been Docherty and that it was not beyond the bounds of possibility that there might be some relationship. Alone in a strange city, Mary Campbell was not going to turn down the offer of friendship from a kinsman when he invited her back to

Old houses in the West Port, near the haunts of Burke and Hare, 1869

his house for breakfast where they could discuss how they might best locate her son.

The Burkes no longer stayed in the Hares' lodging house. They now held the tenancy of a house in Weaver's Close which had been occupied by a cousin of Burke who, for the time being, was away from the city. Helen McDougal made her husband's new acquaintance most welcome while he went in search of Hare. The two returned after the two women had had breakfast and were busy with cleaning. Burke had brought with him provisions and drink enough for a party he proposed holding that evening. There was one problem to be overcome. Lodging at the time with Burke were a Mr and Mrs Gray to whom Burke himself had offered hospitality almost a fortnight previously. The difficulty would be to get this couple out of the house without their being suspicious. He explained that he had discovered that Mrs Docherty was a relative of his wife and since he felt obliged to accommodate her for a day or two, he would be most grateful if they could find alternative lodging for a short while till she went back to Ireland. He even went out to find them the alternative accommodation—the house of Hare and his wife.

That evening, Mrs Hare joined the company and as the whisky flowed, so the enjoyment became noisier, causing neighbours to seek moderation on at least one occasion. Around eleven o'clock, a quarrel started between Burke and Hare, most likely staged like that which had preceded Mary Paterson's death. Tipsy as she was, Mary Campbell intervened to restore harmony but she got knocked down in the fracas. She fell heavily and was unable to get up again. The fighting finished abruptly. Burke and Hare set to work on the prostrate woman in their usual manner. But, a fatal mistake was made. One of them grasped her violently by the throat and left the mark of the undue pressure. Mary Campbell's body was undressed and laid on a quantity of straw lying beside the bed. The carousing resumed and continued until the early hours of the morning.

The next day, Burke called round to Hare's house to see how his erstwhile lodgers fared. The Grays could see little prospect of breakfast being offered by Hare and readily accepted Burke's invitation to eat with him. They wondered why Mrs Docherty was no longer there, but were told that there had been an argument between her and Burke resulting in her being put out and exhorted not to return. Mrs Gray, in particular, was suspicious and later in the day, when only she and her husband were in, conducted a search of the house. She made the grim find of Mary Campbell's body just as Helen McDougal returned. Her landlady implored them not to tell what they had seen. Meanwhile, Burke and Hare were out making arrangements for delivery of their latest victim to Dr Knox. When they returned with the anatomist's porter and a tea-chest, there was no hint that their evil secret may have been discovered or that Mr Gray was away, as he had threatened to Helen Mcdougal, to lodge his information at the police office.

It was some time before Gray was able to see an officer with the authority to act on his information. It was around seven o'clock in the evening before Sergeant-Major Fisher arrived and could take his statement. His first reaction was that he had before him a lodger who had taken an evil disposition towards his landlord. Still, he thought it prudent to attend Burke's house in the West Port. Despite some suspicious findings, Fisher was still unconvinced but was cautious enough to apprehend Burke and McDougal. Later, accompanied by his superior officer and the police surgeon, he returned to the Burkes' house where a more thorough search uncovered *prima facie* evidence that a crime may well have been committed.

Next morning, we know not on what premise, Dr Knox's offices in Surgeon's Square were visited. The body of Mary Campbell, identified by Mr Gray, was found still bundled up in the tea-chest used to carry her from the West Port. The Hares were arrested on suspicion of complicity.

Despite the evidence of the Grays, the prosecution found themselves facing considerable difficulty putting together a case which would be sufficiently water-tight to secure conviction of all four accused. Much of their evidence, they felt, was circumstantial. The various declarations made by the accused were all contradictory to varying degrees. Even their individual statements showed inconsistencies from one to the next. The cunning of Hare, ever with an eye to the main chance, caused him to fully realise that the prosecution were in a quandary. He offered to turn King's evidence on the condition of an assurance that he and his wife would be given an amnesty freeing them from prosecution. The Lord Advocate agonised over his decision for some time but realised that accepting this offer was the only way out of his difficulty. On 8th December, 1828, Burke and McDougal had a citation served on them 'charging them to appear before the High Court of Justiciary, to be held at Edinburgh on Wednesday, the 24th December, at ten o'clock-forenoon, to underlie the law for the crime of murder.' They were indicted for the murders of Mary Paterson, James Wilson and Mary Campbell. The list of witnesses carried the names of fifty people and forty five people were summoned for jury service. During the course of the preliminary arguments and submissions, Burke's counsel stated on his client's behalf that he thought he would suffer prejudice by going to trial on three unconnected murder charges. Their lordships on the bench concurred and the Crown accordingly decided to proceed only on the murder for which they had the most substantive evidence, that of Mary Campbell. The Lord Advocate also indicated that they would proceed with the charge of being art and part of the crime against

Helen McDougal. Had Burke not proceeded with his claim, it is likely that McDougal would have been released, for the evidence against her on the first two murder charges was very thin indeed and the weakness of the case could well have influenced the jury in her favour on the third charge.

The court was packed to hear the evidence to be put forward by the prosecution. In particular, all wished to hear what the Hares had to say. William Hare had to tread a very thin line. As the trial judge, Lord Meadowbank, told him, 'Whatever share you may have had in the transaction, if you now speak the truth, you can never afterwards be questioned in a court of justice,' but if he were to prevaricate he could be assured of full retribution. He gave an account of the events leading to Mary Campbell's death, being very careful not to incriminate himself. It was his cross-examination which was likely to be his greatest test. Henry Cockburn (later to become the renowned judge, Lord Cockburn), counsel for McDougal, asked him if he had 'been connected in supplying the doctors with subjects upon other occasions.' The Lord Advocate objected on the grounds that the witness should not be questioned on any other matter than the case being tried. This presented a difficult point of law with authorities being cited on both sides. With typical legal compromise, the judges decided that such questions could be put, but that the witness was not bound to answer any question which might incriminate him. This, of course, made Hare's position even more difficult. To a man of the eloquence of Cockburn, it was an extremely attractive challenge to phrase his questions in such a way that the witness had to be very cautious in making reply and the length of his hesitations sufficient to imply, for the benefit of the jury, the responses Cockburn was seeking. Uncomfortable as he must have felt, Hare's original evidence was in no way shaken by the grilling he received.

Once evidence had been led, the Lord Advocate, Sir William Rae, immediately addressed the jury on what he described as 'one of the most extraordinary and novel subjects of trial ever brought before this or any other court.' His speech was attended with great interest, dealing as it did with many important issues not just of criminal activity but of legal precedent. It was acknowledged to be one of the best he had ever made. By comparison, the Dean of the Faculty was very laboured, much of his rhetoric being directed at Hare and his reliability as a credible witness. Cockburn was at his brilliant best. He shrewdly put it to the jury that they did have the option of finding his client's case not proven if they could not bring themselves to acquit her but at the same time were not wholly convinced of her guilt.

The jury retired at 8.30 a.m. on Christmas day, the trial having continued since 10 a.m. the previous day. After an absence of fifty minutes, they returned for the foreman to give the verdict, 'The jury find the pannel, William Burke, guilty of the third charge of the indictment; and find the indictment not proven against the pannel, Helen McDougal.'

The Lord-Advocate moved for sentence. According to the *Edinburgh Evening Courtant*, 'The scene was altogether awful and impressive. The prisoner stood up with unshaken firmness. Not a muscle of his features was discomposed during the solemn address of the Lord Justice Clerk consigning him to his doom. The female prisoner was much agitated, and was drowned in tears during the whole course of the melancholy process.'

Addressing McDougal, the Right Hon. David Boyle, Lord Justice-Clerk said, 'You know whether you have been in the commission of this atrocious crime. I leave it to your own conscience to draw the proper conclusion. I hope and trust that you will betake yourself to a new line of life, diametrically opposite from that which you have lead for a number of years.'

Assuming the black cap, he addressed Burke passing the customary sentence and adding the following unique provisions, '. . . the only doubt the court entertains of your offence . . . is whether your body should not be exhibited in chains, in order to deter others from the like crimes in time coming. But taking into consideration that the public eye would be offended by so dismal an exhibition, I am disposed to agree that your sentence shall be put into execution in the usual way, but unaccompanied by the statutory attendant of the punishment of the crime of murder—viz, that your body should be publicly dissected and anatomised, and I trust that if ever it is customary to preserve skeletons, yours will be preserved, in order that posterity may keep in remembrance your atrocious crimes.'

While applauding the legal retribution wreaked on Burke, there was great unrest at his fellow conspirators being able to escape scot-free. What ultimately happened to each of them is unknown. All that is certain is that they were pursued and harried to Newcastle, in the case of William Hare and Helen McDougal, and Glasgow in the case of Mary Hare. They appear never to have met up again after leaving Edinburgh.

From two o'clock in the morning of 28th January, defying the rain and the cold, those wishing to witness Burke's execution were beginning to gather around the head of Liberton's Wynd. The enterprising occupants of the tenements overlooking the scaffold sold positions at their windows for prices varying between five and twenty shillings depending on the excellence of the view. By 7 a.m., over 20,000 people had assembled. An hour later, Burke was brought out from his cell in the lock-up adjacent to the appointed place. After completing his devotions, the rope was put round his neck. The knot was adjusted. A white cotton night-cap was pulled over his head. As he recited the Apostles' Creed, the bolt was drawn and the most infamous murderer swung on the gallows to a resounding cheer. The rope was drawn up to bring the body up above the level of the scaffold where it was left to hang for fully three-quarters of an hour.

The body was taken to the university where it was put on display, naked, on a black marble table in the anatomical lecture theatre. It is estimated that, during the day, some 25,000 filed past the body. 'The spectacle was sufficiently ghastly to gratify the most epicurean appetite for horrors.' The body was then taken for dissection and preserving. In accordance with the hopes of the Lord Justice-Clerk, Burke's skeleton can be seen to this day in the Anatomy Museum of the university's medical school.

Execution of Burke

A POISONER'S DECEPTIONS

The murder of Elizabeth Chantrelle, 1878

The trial of Eugene Marie Chantrelle, accused of murdering his wife by administering her with poison, occupies a position of some prominence in Scottish legal history. The apparent social position of the accused and the strange catalogue of circumstances leading up to the crime and the equally unusual circumstances attending the conviction make the case as interesting as the later one of the infamous Dr Pritchard in Scotland's second city. Much of the evidence was purely circumstantial. Taken in isolation, the events would be dismissed as happenstance. But in combination, they were accepted as adequate proof of Chantrelle's guilt.

Chantrelle was born in Nantes, in France, in 1834, the son of a prominent shipowner. He had an excellent education including a period of medical studies at the medical school in his home town. Despite his ability, he had to discontinue his studies there through lack of adequate finances—a state owing much to his father's misfortunes at the time of the French Revolution. He was, however, later able to resume studies in Strasbourg and Paris, though it seems that the liking he had acquired in the interim for the more social activities of life detracted from his academic pursuits.

Having acquired communist tendencies, Napoleonic France held no attractions for Chantrelle and he crossed the Channel. Being an excellent linquist and having acquired a polished, cultured mien as a result of his

education, he readily found positions as a teacher of French. This new profession brought him to Edinburgh in 1866 where many of the leading educational establishments employed his services. Amongst them was a private school known as Newington Academy, where he first met the fifteen year old Elizabeth Dyer. Unfortunately, the relationship between teacher and pupil grew rather more intimate than it properly should. It is not difficult to understand the attractions, one for the other, of a very attractive young woman and a debonair Frenchman. Elizabeth Dyer fell pregnant. In order to protect her reputation, Chantrelle agreed to marry the girl though, at sixteen, Elizabeth Dyer seemed less anxious than her parents for the proposed union. Nevertheless, the couple were married on 11th August, 1868, and two months later, the first of their four children was born.

That Chantrelle had any real affection for his reluctant bride is doubtful. Even before her first confinement, he had begun his physical and mental ill-treatment of her. Frequently during their married life, Elizabeth had to seek refuge with her mother and on at least two occasions, the police had to be called for her protection. Chantrelle made her the butt of his blasphemies, would strike her, threaten her and was callously and openly unfaithful to her. One of his most oft uttered threats was that of poisoning her, declaring that he had enough knowledge of matters medical that he could readily put effect to his boast without fear of detection. Only her love of her children prevented Elizabeth Chantrelle from leaving her prison of misery. Although she did, on one occasion, consult a solicitor with a view to obtaining a divorce, her sensitive nature caused her to shrink back from the inevitable exposure. At that time, divorce was not an action to be lightly prosecuted.

In due course, Chantrelle's increasing use of drink and his more abusive tendencies began to take their toll on his professional as well as his private life. The demand for his skills waned and he fell into considerable financial difficulties. He desperately required to find some way of raising money. Although he had frequently threatened his wife's life, it is unlikely that he had any intention of carrying his threats through into practice until his impoverishment suggested this as a way of obtaining money.

In October, 1877, he made application to become an agent of the Star Accidental Assurance Company. This enabled him to make extensive investigations into what constituted accidental death for the purpose of insurance. He then took out policies with the Accidental Assurance Association of Scotland providing for £1000 to be paid on the accidental death of himself or his wife. Elizabeth Chantrelle was very much against a policy on her own life being effected. She showed even greater apprehension for her safety, remarking to her mother that she feared her death may be the more imminent now that her husband could financially gain from it.

Chantrelle now applied himself to designing a plan which would, firstly, make the death of his wife a certainty and would, secondly, ensure that it was put down to an accident. Drawing on his medical knowledge, he decided on the use of a narcotic which would leave no trace in the body to secure the first object and to provide that the death appeared to have been caused by coal-gas poisoning to secure the second.

On New Year's Day, 1878, Madame Chantrelle gave her maid, Mary Byrne, a holiday while the whole family remained at their home in George Street. Elizabeth cooked the family's dinner which was much enjoyed by all, but during the course of the afternoon she began to feel unwell. She was sick at least once and went off to bed soon after six o'clock. Mary Byrne returned around ten o'clock to find her mistress looking very heavy. She helped her to drink some lemonade and to eat part of an orange which were lying on a table beside her bed. From the state of the bedclothes, Mary gained the impression that Elizabeth had been very restless. Mary Byrne straightened up the room and ensured that the gas fire was safely lit before retiring to her own room. She heard nothing more that night save the noise of the baby being comforted by one of the elder children as he was being carried from Elizabeth Chantrelle's room to that occupied by the children and their father.

The next morning, the maid rose at seven o'clock to hear moaning coming from her mistress's room, the door of which was ajar. She found her lying unconscious with evidence of vomit on the bedclothes and in her hair. The fire no longer burned but there was no smell of gas. She immediately called for Chantrelle who tried to rouse his wife. Mary Byrne went out to attend to the baby whom Chantrelle said he thought was crying. When she returned, Chantrelle made remark on the smell of gas. At first she did not notice it, but gradually became more and more aware of it until it became so strong that she went to shut off the supply at the meter. Chantrelle summoned the family doctor, Dr Carmichael, who noticed the very strong smell of gas and he in turn summoned Dr Littlejohn, the City Medical Officer, to see a case of coal-gas poisoning, apparently a rare occurrence. Initially, both doctors were of the opinion that Elizabeth was dying and should be removed to the Royal Infirmary. The affirmations of Chantrelle and the evidence of their noses did not raise any doubts in their minds as to the cause of the patient's imminent death.

Careful examination of the patient on admission by Professor Maclagan suggested to him that the symptoms were more consistent with narcotic poisoning. Elizabeth Chantrelle died that afternoon without regaining consciousness. On the following day, a post-mortem was conducted on the orders of the procurator-fiscal. The results were inconclusive, though it was confirmed that death was not caused by coal-gas poisoning. Certain organs were removed for chemical analysis, but this equally cast no light on the cause of death, there being no sign of any poisonous substance present. The authorities' disquiet heightened and again the scene of the suspected crime was visited for a closer scrutiny. A fracture was discovered in a gas pipe behind the window shutter in Elizabeth Chantrelle's bedroom. Subsequent examination showed that this could not have been caused other than deliberately, though Chantrelle denied knowledge of the pipe's very existence. This denial was provably false. In addition, bedclothes taken from Elizabeth's bed were removed for examination of vomit stains. The nightclothes worn by the patient on her admission to the Royal Infirmary were also obtained to be subjected to the same examination. Of particular interest were some dark brown stains. Maceration of the pieces of material carrying these stains in water gave solutions which smelled of opium and gave positive chemical tests for one of the principle components of the substance. On the basis of this evidence, application was later made for the exhumation of the body in order to undertake detailed tests on the digestive system of the victim. Still no trace of opium or any poisonous vegetable materials could be found.

Chantrelle was arrested immediately after his wife's funeral on 5th January and taken to Calton Gaol to await trial on 8th April. That he had to wait so long attested to the care with which the prosecution had to build up and prepare its case given the lack of any proof positive. Their case rested on the unlikelihood of suicide, the medical symptoms of narcotic poisoning, the presence of opium residues in vomit stains, Chantrelle's acquaintance with poisons, his purchase of a quantity of opium extract, the fractured gas pipe and the gas leak, the attitude of the accused towards his wife and the somewhat strange protestations of innocence made by Chantrelle even before any charge had been levelled at him.

The defence had a difficult task despite the circumstantial nature of the prosecution's evidence. The tack adopted had to be negative, that there was no absolute proof that Chantrelle had administered poison to his wife. Chantrelle was not called to the witness box. Only after his trial did he make any statement on his own behalf. He tried to demolish the whole prosecution case by arguing that his wife had taken opium voluntarily and that some person unknown had incriminated him by rubbing the poison into his wife's linen. He appeared not to appreciate that he was also demolishing his own original claim that coal-gas poisoning was the cause of his wife's death.

Chantrelle was found guilty and duly sentenced to be executed on 31st May. His was the first execution in the capital in accordance with the Capital Punishment Amendment Act of 1868 which provided that sentences would no longer be open to public view. Despite an appeal to the Home Secretary and attempts to mobilise public support for the unsoundness of the conviction, the procession to the scaffold was formed at eight o'clock on the morning of the appointed day. A short walk took them to an outhouse which had been adapted for the purpose. The floor of this outhouse formed the ceiling to a deep cellar beneath, and into this floor was cut a hole four feet square, closed off by a trap door comprising two parts held in place by a bolt. The scaffold was constructed of two uprights and a crossbeam to which was attached the hook to which in turn, the hangman's rope was attached. Chantrelle dispassionately eyed the sombre room as he entered. He took his place on the trap-door and submitted to the final adjustment of the rope round his neck. While the minister intoned the Lord's Prayer, the bolt clicked back and Chantrelle fell eight feet to his instantaneous death. To the end he had maintained his innocence, making no indication of any kind that could be construed as a confession of guilt. However, even if his innocence on this particular charge had been accepted by the court, there is a strong indication that the Crown was prepared to indict him on another capital charge.

———————

THE STOCKBRIDGE BABY FARMER

The case of Jessie King, 1889

'Jessie Kean or King, the Stockbridge baby farmer, was executed yesterday morning within the Calton Jail, Edinburgh. There was no scene at the scaffold. The woman showed the greatest composure in meeting her doom. Berry, of Bradford, was the executioner. King left a supplementary confession, which was taken to London yesterday, and will be in the hands of the Scottish Secretary today.' Thus, the *Scotsman* of Tuesday 12th March, 1889 tersely announced the execution of the last woman to suffer such a fate in Edinburgh. Although her crimes caused revulsion amongst the people of the city, at the same time she attracted much sympathy, even to the extent of a petition being drawn up to try to gain a reprieve for her. However, she seems to have been equally able of exciting the opposite emotion, one eye-witness to her trial describing her as 'mean, furtive; shabbily furtive, like a cornered rat.' Whatever the personal characteristics or circumstances which caused Jessie King to perpetrate her crimes, her case opened a window on life as it then was in certain social levels of the city. It showed that it was quite common for parents to sell their children for a few pounds with little regard for what became of them. Nevertheless, we cannot truly criticise or judge them at this distance in time, for few now can have any conception of the depth of poverty which then existed and the heavy burden of trying to satisfy another mouth from already overstretched resources.

Little or nothing is known of Jessie King's early life. The period of her life which was to bring her notoriety began in May 1887, when she took up with a man by the name of Pearson. At first, they lived in Gifford Park but soon moved to a house in the nearby Dalkeith Road. The couple appeared to be reasonably happy together, only on occasion having mild arguments, though witnesses at King's trial claimed to have seen her suffering from the effects of drink. On occasion, the possibility of adopting a child was discussed, but with no definite commitments being made until, in November, King saw an advertisement for a baby boy, five months old, for whom adoptive parents were being sought.

Walter Anderson Campbell was born in Prestonpans on 20th May, 1887, to Elizabeth Campbell, a worker in the local wire works. As so frequently happened in past ages, soon after the birth, complications developed in the mother which were to prove fatal within a week. Before she died, however, she was able to reveal to her sister that the baby's father was a man by the name of David Finlay from Leith. The sister took care of the orphaned child for about three months until his father decided that the child should be adopted. Amongst those approaching him was Jessie King. She claimed that she had recently lost a baby of about the same age and that she had been in low spirits since then. Finlay was easily taken in by her story and agreed to let her have the child. He paid her the sum of £5 and the following day she and her 'husband' collected Walter from his foster parents in Prestonpans.

King and Pearson appeared to neighbours to be devoted parents. Pearson in particular grew to be very fond of the boy. However, one day he returned home to find Walter missing. Wondering where he was, Jessie told Pearson that she had taken him to Miss Stirling's Home for Orphans because she had grown tired of him. the story she gave to the neighbours was that she had only been keeping Walter on a temporary basis and that he had returned to his own mother, Jessie's sister. The neighbours did not question the story because, strange as it may seem, within that particular tenement, the inhabitants tended to keep themselves very much to themselves and had no other knowledge of the circumstances of Walter's life which would have caused them to be suspicious. It is difficult to imagine how Jessie was able to keep her guilty secret from Pearson without his becoming suspicious, particularly on the occasion he decided that he would like to visit his adopted son whom he missed. She explained that men were only infrequently admitted to the home in Causewayside and it was unlikely that he would be allowed to see Walter. It did not seem to register with Pearson that there was no such home in Causewayside. Miss Stirling's was to be found in Stockbridge. Neither Pearson nor anybody else ever saw Walter Campbell again.

In May 1887, Catherine Gunn, an unmarried domestic servant, gave birth to twin sons, Alexander and Robert. Finding she was unable to keep the children, she fostered them out to a woman in Rose Street. The boys thrived but after eleven months, their mother found she could no longer keep up the weekly payments and through the nurse who had attended her at her confinement, she advertised the boys for adoption. In the meantime, King and Pearson had moved to Stockbridge, taking rooms under the name of Macpherson with a Mrs Mackenzie in Ann's Court. Jessie King was one of the two successful applicants from the twenty-eight people who answered the advertisement. She was given the stronger of the two boys, Alexander, along with an adoption fee of £3. She had been sufficiently confident of obtaining one of the twins to have told Mrs Mackenzie in advance of his arrival that she was expecting the son of her husband's sister who had been taken ill and had asked that she care for him while she was in the Royal Infirmary. She made the strange representation that her brother was married to her sister-in-law, presumably in the hope that such a strange situation could only be accepted as true and would prevent too many searching questions being asked of her.

During the day, Jessie King worked in the local laundry but she was fortunate in having a young girl a few doors away who was very fond of Alexander and was more than pleased to look after him until King came home each evening. One day, however, on going to collect her ward, she was told that her services would no longer be required because Alexander's father had come the previous evening to take him home. Jessie King explained that her sister-in-law had died and that, although he could not properly look after the boy himself, his father considered that he could not inconvenience Jessie any longer, so intended to make more permanent provision for Alexander's future. A few weeks later, Alexander's natural mother called to see him as she had done on a few previous occasions, only to find that the Macphersons had moved house. None of the neighbours made any link between this woman and the young Alexander.

Violet Tomlinson was born in August 1888. Like Alexander Gunn, her mother was in domestic service. Her grandmother looked after her until she could be adopted but unfortunately for Violet, Jessie King was again chosen as the adoptive mother. She offered to take Violet for just £2, explaining that the baby was for her sister who was married to one of the Duke of Montrose's pipers. She was unable to have children herself and desperately wanted to adopt a baby. Hence she was not interested in seeking any significant fee from the child's parents. On the day in late September on which she collected Violet, Jessie King claimed that her sister happened to be in Edinburgh and was excited at the prospect of returning home that afternoon with her newly adopted daughter. Jessie King was actually seen to return with the baby to the house in Cheyne Street she and Pearson had occupied since leaving Ann's Court in June. But no one ever saw Violet alive again. Pearson did not even know that his wife had been seeking another child let alone brought one home. Again, nobody seemed to express undue concern at the disappearance of the baby—a serious indictment of a social system which seemed to accept the buying and selling of young children as part and parcel of everyday life. Those who had shown no suspicions were to be rudely awakened by a grisly find in Cheyne Street on the afternoon of Friday 26th October, 1888.

Around half past one, some boys were playing in Cheyne Street when they found a parcel rolled up in a waterproof coat in one of the back yards. Thinking it was just an old pair of boots to be thrown out, they started to kick it around. Two of the boys, however, were more curious. They started to unwrap it but their stomachs turned on finding what it contained. Inside, was the badly decomposed body of a young child. They immediately reported their find to the local constable who conveyed the parcel and its contents to the mortuary. Dr Littlejohn, the city's medical officer, found the body to be that of a boy about a year old. It was wrapped in an oilskin cloth presenting the appearance of a mummy. A ligature ran round its neck twice and was embedded in the skin. The body was too far decomposed to determine the cause of death but strangulation was a reasonable assumption.

During the subsequent enquiries, Detective James Clark learned of the unannounced appearance and equally sudden disappearance of Violet Tomlinson the previous month. He decided to question Jessie King who gave him the story of her sister on the Duke of Montrose's estate. Despite the discrepancy in ages and the differing sexes of the body found and the Tomlinson baby, Clark's suspicions were aroused. He considered a search of the house to be in order. In a coal-closet normally kept locked by King, and which she had tried to prevent him from opening, the detective found a small body wrapped in canvas cloth. He locked up the house and took King and the body to the police station. He returned to the house to conduct a more thorough search. On the topmost shelf of the closet, he found a mark corresponding to the body of a child and some scraps of material which appeared to be the same as that which had been wrapped around the body found by the young boys. Dr Littlejohn confirmed that the material was the same and also that the second body was that of a young female child who had been strangled. King was promptly charged with the murders of Alexander Gunn and Violet Tomlinson.

In her confession, King admitted that she had taken the Gunn boy in April for the sum of £3, but by the end of May found she could no longer afford to support him. She had tried, without success, to have him admitted to Miss Stirling's Home. In despair, she had returned home and, while her husband had been out of the house, strangled the boy. She wrapped the body in a cloth and put it in a box in a cupboard. There it remained until she moved it with all her other effects to Stockbridge. The body had been kept in a cellar until a fortnight previously when she wrapped it in the oilskin cloth and dumped it on a piece of waste ground not fifty yards from her house. As for Violet Tomlinson, her life in King's house had lasted but hours. Shortly after bringing her home, King had given the baby some whisky to keep it quiet. However, the whisky must have been stronger than she had thought, for it took the baby's breath away and it lay gasping for air. She put her hand over Violet's mouth and choked her. She tied a cloth over the baby's mouth to ensure that she would not revive and put the body in the cellar where Detective Clark was to find it.

Continuing his enquiries, Clark went further back into King's barbarous history. Pearson was to prove a useful witness for his investigations, being an innocent accomplice completely ignorant of his wife's dark secrets. He recounted the story of Walter Campbell, causing Clark to initiate a search of their previous lodgings in Dalkeith Road. However, even lifting floor-boards furnished no evidence of Walter's fate. Nevertheless, a third charge of murder was laid against King, though the Solicitor-General subsequently withdrew from prosecuting her on his charge for insufficiency of evidence.

Jessie King was brought to trial at the High Court of Justiciary on 18th February, 1889. The prosecution led its evidence but the defence could do little against the incontrovertible facts of the case. The best that Mr Fitzroy Bell could do on behalf of his client was try to shift some of the blame on to those parents who sold their children; so far as moral responsibility was concerned, he argued, they were not without their share. He also suggested that King might have been acting under the influence and control of Pearson. However, his entreaties were all to no avail. After retiring at three o'clock for just a few minutes, the jury returned a guilty verdict. The verdict was officially recorded and signed by the Lord Justice-Clerk. He addressed the prisoner slowly and tremulously:

'Jessie King, no one who has listened to the evidence of this trial could fail to be satisfied that the jury could come to no other conclusion than that which they have come to in your case. Your days are now numbered. Remember, the sentence of this Court, the penalty of the law and the sentence relate to this world and to this world only. Do, I entreat you, be persuaded not to harden your heart against the world to come. All that you have done can be blotted out for the world to come if you will be repent and turn from it. Listen, I beseech you, to the ministrations you will receive, and as you confessed your crime in your declaration to man, so confess it also to God, and you will be sure of forgiveness.'

When his Lordship put on the black cap to deliver sentence, King turned ghostly white and then gave vent to heart-rending groans. When he concluded with the customary words, 'This is pronounced for doom and may the Lord have mercy on your soul', the agony of her face distressed even the hardest of hearts. She was taken in a fainting condition down the stair to the cells and from there to Calton Jail to await the day of her execution.

NOT PROVEN

The death of Mrs Bertha Merrett, 1926

Virtually every system of criminal justice in the world permits only two verdicts in its trials of those accused of having transgressed the law. The notable exception is the system in Scotland which allows not only for black and white but a shade of grey in between—the verdict of 'not proven'. Few concepts can have attracted more discussion or controversy, particularly if one adopts the cynics' view that the shade of grey is fairly dark, the imputation of such a verdict being 'We know you did it, but go away and don't do it again.' Fortunately, the verdict is not often returned. However, when it is, it can turn a crime and the subsequent trial into something of a sensation. Though it might equally be claimed that there was already something peculiar about the case for the jury to feel obliged to find the accused 'not proven'. One of the celebrated cases in which the jury could not find itself able to return a definitive verdict was that of the alleged murder of Mrs Bertha Merrett by her son, John Donald Merrett, in 1926.

Donald Merrett was born in New Zealand, the son of an electrical engineer. While he was still young, the family moved to Russia but the climate did not agree with him and just before the outbreak of war, he and his mother, Bertha Merrett, were sent to Switzerland. There were already signs of increasing disenchantment in the relationship between Donald's parents, and, as it happened, the family were never again to be reunited. In 1924, mother and son came to England to complete his education at Malvern College. He left the college in December 1925 under a slight cloud on account of an

incident which might easily be attributed to youthful exuberance. However, it was enough to cause uneasiness in his mother so that instead of allowing him to go up to Oxford, she decided that he attend the non-resident University of Edinburgh where he could stay at home and she could keep an eye on him. They moved from their rented cottage near Reading to Edinburgh in January 1926. After a few weeks in rooms, they rented a flat at 31 Buckingham Terrace.

Neighbours all considered Mrs Merrett to be a very pleasant woman with much personal charm and the social graces which made her an acceptable newcomer to this affluent part of the town. She appeared to be devoted to her son, being concerned for his success and future almost to the exclusion of her own needs and comforts. Yet, this adulation was not returned. Perhaps as a reaction against her over-powering attentiveness, Donald took to deceiving his mother. He had duly enrolled at his classes and paid the fees, but after only six weeks he ceased attending, though he continued to leave the house each morning with his books, to all intents and purposes, heading for his first lecture of the day. His evenings too were not all they seemed.

After dinner each evening since embarking on his course, he had taken himself to his room to study. After a few weeks, he claimed to be suffering from occasional sleep walking. Concerned for his safety lest during one of his sojourns he might fall from his first floor window, his mother agreed that a rope should be tied across his window. However, the only way he was liable to go out through his window was by his own conscious volition, down the very rope which was meant to restrain him. He had made the acquaintance of Betty Christie and George Scott, both instructors at the Dunedin Palais de Danse in Picardy Place, and was regularly 'booking out' Miss Christie at thirty shillings a night or fifteen shillings an afternoon. He found this to be an infinitely more amenable way of spending time than poring over his books. Mrs Merrett was blissfully unaware of his extra-curricular activities. She still firmly believed that her son was an exemplary student who exhibited considerable diligence to his studies each evening and who never missed a scheduled class each day.

Mrs Merrett's annual income from her investments was £700, but as her son grew older and the cost of living increased, she found it more difficult to keep up their accustomed standard of living. She allowed Donald ten shillings a week but required him to account for every penny. And yet, she did not seem to exercise the same standards of book-keeping across all her accounts, otherwise she might have made more early discovery of the fact that she was paying for a much more extravagant lifestyle for her son's personal enjoyment than 10s. a week could buy. Despite her predilection for being thrifty, she still felt that she could afford a daily help, though this may only have been for appearances' sake. Each day, just before nine o'clock, Henrietta Sutherland would arrive for the morning's work which was to keep her until midday. She was a pleasant young woman who was separated from her husband and supported herself from such jobs as she could obtain as a domestic help.

On the morning of 13th March, Mrs Merrett was surprised to receive a letter from her bank manager informing her that her current account was in danger of becoming overdrawn. She was advised to make an appropriate transfer from her deposit accounts. She decided that she ought to investigate the matter but before she could arrange an interview at her bank, she received another letter, on 16th March, confirming that the account now stood overdrawn. The matter troubled her all day and that night she decided she must discuss the matter with her son, though there is no way of telling whether she actually suspected him of being directly responsible for the irregularities. She would raise it with him the next morning.

On the morning of 17th March, Henrietta Sutherland arrived as normal. Mrs Merrett seemed her usual self. The breakfast table was cleared with still no mention of matters financial. Mrs Merrett went to her writing desk to write some letters while her son sat in an armchair reading a book. Mrs Sutherland reset the table ready for lunch and made her way back to the kitchen to clean and re-kindle the fire there. Suddenly, she thought she heard a gunshot and jumped to her feet, uncertain what to do. Before she could resolve her indecision, Donald Merrett appeared at the kitchen door, looking very distressed, and told her that his mother had shot herself. He said that she had questioned him about his wasting money and a quarrel had developed when she quite unexpectedly drew a gun from her desk, held it to her head and pulled the trigger.

Mrs Sutherland and Merrett went through to the sitting room to find Mrs Merrett lying unconscious on the floor, blood pouring from a wound behind her right ear, an upturned chair lay beside her. A pistol was lying on the bureau. During the subsequent investigations, it was discovered that Merrett had bought the weapon, so he claimed, because he and his mother had intended to go abroad at Easter and wished to carry some insurance of safety.

Mrs Sutherland's first thought was to telephone the

police rather than to summon medical help, though she gave no hint that she suspected foul play. The police brought an ambulance with them which promptly conveyed Mrs Merrett to the Royal Infirmary. Since circumstances were suggestive of attempted suicide, she was consigned to Ward 3 with its barred windows and locked doors. Unfortunately, this course of action conspired to conceal the truth of what had happened in the Merretts' sitting room. Because attempted suicide was an offence, no one was allowed to give Mrs Merrett any indication of the true reason for her being in hospital or to directly question her on the cause of her injury other than the police officers who, for a variety of reasons, had already convinced themselves of the veracity of Merrett's claim that his mother had shot herself.

During her stay in hospital, Mrs Merrett slowly recalled certain parts of the fateful morning's events. She claimed to Sister Grant that she had been at her desk writing a letter, her son standing beside her waiting to take the letter to the post-office, when she heard a bang in her ear like a pistol. She made similar comments to other members of the medical staff and to her visitors. Still the police's beliefs were not seriously undermined and they took little or no action. Mrs Merrett's protestations became more and more definite, with more and more of the background being painted in detail as her memory returned. She was still critically ill and nine days after the shot which had felled her, she became delirious and then comatose. She died in the early hours of 1st April. The certified cause of death was given as 'basal meningitis, following a bullet wound in the cranium.' A post-mortem was held later the same day, the pathologist's conclusion being that there was 'nothing to indicate a distance at which the discharge took place . . . so far as the position of the wound is concerned, the case is consistent with suicide.' He also found difficulty in attributing her death to accident, but suggested that such a possibility should not be excluded. Merrett's claims were vindicated — or were they?

Merrett's behaviour during his mother's fight for life

fell somewhat short of what might have been expected of an only son. Though she missed him and often asked for him, he only infrequently visited his mother. He much preferred the enjoyment to be found in Miss Christie's company. His one apparent concession was to move into the County Hotel in Lothian road, just five minutes walk from the hospital, though the more cynical would suggest that his intention was to be more able to entertain Miss Christie without incurring the undue attentions of his neighbours in Buckingham Terrace.

Amongst Mrs Merrett's visitors was her sister, Mrs Penn, and her husband who had come north from Brighton. At Mrs Merrett's insistence, Mr and Mrs Penn stayed in the flat in Buckingham Terrace where, on the day before Mrs Merrett's death, they found a spent cartridge case. They were totally unconvinced by the claims of attempted suicide and called in the police. Only now was a more thorough investigation begun. Certain documents and a box of .38 calibre cartridges were removed for examination. A more rigorous interview with Donald Merrett was conducted to try to build up a picture of the events leading up to the shot being fired from the pistol. The investigating officer remained unenlightened, but harboured unsubstantiated suspicions. He would need to await forensic examination of the items he had removed. Unfortunately these were inconclusive.

In the middle of April, Merrett announced to his aunt, with whom he was now staying back at Buckingham Terrace, that he was going to London to consult with a famous detective. What he omitted to tell her was that he was going in the company of two young ladies, one of whom was under the age of consent. This should have raised some questions in the police mind, but still they exhibited extreme reticence to move. It was not until late November, after Merrett had been to London and returned, and had subsequently moved to live in Buckinghamshire, that a petition was presented to the Sheriff of the Lothians and Peebles for grant of warrant for Merrett's apprehension on charges of murdering his mother and uttering forged cheques. His trial on indictment began on 1st February. That he did come to trial owed rather more to the persistence of Mrs Merrett's bankers pursuing their own investigations into the irregularities of her account than to any diligence on the part of the police whose official line was still that Mrs Merrett had taken her own life.

The prominent feature of the trial was the wealth of legal talent and the panoply of expert witnesses summoned to support both prosecution and defence. The capital's police force had made a poor showing in their handling of the case from the start and would be well aware of the Crown's annoyance at trying to find substantive and sustainable evidence of detail, so long after the event. Their case was made no easier by the fact that Merrett exercised his prerogative of not entering the witness box. Remember that he was the only person present at the moment of the fatal gunshot.

The charges relating to the forged cheques could be relatively easily proven on the basis of evidence from hand writing experts. The highlight awaited by all showing interest in the trial was the much publicised confrontation between the two forensic heavyweights of the age, Professor John Glaister and Sir Bernard Spilsbury. To them was essentially given the task of deciding the murder charge by setting forth their opposing opinions on the tenability of suicide. As might have been predicted, the event, after its build-up, was an anti-climax. It was a very gentlemanly exposition of the differing opinions which may be derived from substantially the same tests carried out in different laboratories. The case, despite the weight of pleading and peripheral evidence, had come down to consideration of powder or burning marks which might be expected from the weapon fired at a target at close range. Closer and more detailed examination than the original post mortem had provided for led the prosecution witnesses to be firmly of the opinion that suicide or accidental self-shooting were quite out of the question. But Spilsbury, a stubborn and dogmatic man, held exactly the opposite view. However, his experiments were shown to be worthless because he had only employed a weapon of similar type, not the actual gun by which Mrs Merrett had died. The trial judge warned the jury of this, but in the layman, a clash of scientific experts can easily cause scepticism and rejection of both views as valid evidence.

The jury retired at 4.35 p.m. on the seventh day of the trial and within an hour, returned with a verdict of guilty on the charge of uttering false cheques and not proven on the charge of murder. Merrett was sent to prison for twelve months. At the end of the day, he had escaped a death sentence through the incompetence of the police and the misleading evidence of Spilsbury who had made a mistake and was too proud, or stubborn, to admit it.

There were many who thought that this would not be the last time that Merrett would find himself at odds with the law. How right they were to prove. After his discharge from prison, he found smuggling, gun-running and gambling to be very lucrative pursuits and soon established an enviable lifestyle. At the outbreak of war, he joined the Royal Navy seeing the senior service as that most likely to be of benefit to his personal pursuits. He continued his nefarious practices through and after the war until he became known to the police in many countries. In 1954, he conceived a plan to murder his wife and so obtain a sum he had settled on her when he had finally inherited his mother's estate. His plan well matched his flamboyant personality. But, unfortunately for him, his mother-in-law caught him during its execution and her necessary death made his wife's death appear not to be the accident he had intended it to look. He did manage to escape but step by step, the police closed in on him. Yet again, however, he successfully eluded the hangman's rope. Aware that his arrest was imminent, he walked out one night into a nearby wood and, ironically, shot himself through the head.
